THE COLLECTIVE:10 PLAY ANTHOLOGY
VOLUME 2

I0078467

THE COLLECTIVE
TEN MINUTE PLAY FEST

12 original short plays

VOLUME 2

edited by **Robert Z Grant**
and **Lisa Kicielinski**

The dialogue starts now.

THE COLLECTIVE:10 PLAY ANTHOLOGY, VOLUME 2, 2nd ed., FEBRUARY 2015

Copyright © 2015 by The Collective: Theatre, Arts & Film, Ltd.

Rights reserved. Published in the United States. New York, New York.

Permissions can be found at the end of the book.

Cataloging-in-Publication Data is on file at the Library of Congress.

ISBN: 978-0-9911968-2-1

www.thecollective-ny.org

Printed in the United States of America
10 9 8 7 6 5 4 3

◯:10

CONTENTS

O):IO

Tell me a story.

A tapestry of intimacy and tenderness is woven into that simple request. In asking for a story, one becomes vulnerable – lays open the heart.

Take care of me. Lift me up. Comfort me. Make me laugh. Entertain me. Keep me company. Let me know that I belong – that I am a part of something bigger than myself.

Stories cradle us in childhood and inform us as adults. They tether us to our unremembered pasts and pull us forward into our imagined futures.

Everyone has a story. Some storytellers need a little prompting while others are eager to share. There is a reciprocity in storytelling. The teller simultaneously gives and receives. The telling illuminates the interior landscape of the teller and thus helps to navigate the outer world.

How easy it is to show up with one's joy when working with the storytellers known as The Collective – a group of actors, playwrights and directors that doesn't grab for quick answers, but slowly raises the questions. What is the story? How do I tell it? What is my role in it? How do I serve it? How does it serve mankind? The writer writes and rewrites, the actor explores and lives into the circumstances, and the director watches and suggests and shapes and hones. And then there it is – a living, breathing story.

Congratulations to The Collective on their second NYC production of short plays and this anthology of those stories.

With gratitude and love.

– Susan Aston

Susan Aston works as a teacher, coach and actress in NYC. She has appeared on Broadway and in film and television and is a member of The Actors Studio. She has coached Emmy-, SAG-, Tony-, and Golden Globe-Award winning performances and was honored by The Academy of Television Arts and Sciences, 2003 Emmys, for Contribution to the Performance of James Gandolfini, Best Actor, HBO, The Sopranos.

Collective:10 continued this year as one way to find and develop relationships with writers. The number of submissions more than tripled this year. The increased numbers created a glut of reading that felt as if it was clouding the process, but ultimately produced the thirteen gems published in this volume.

Our submission process is blind. That means, even for writers whose work we already know and love, every play gets a fair chance at being selected for the festival. However, one of the unexpected outcomes of the blind process is that ALL of our playwrights last year were white males. We took flack about our lack of women and racially diverse writers and took steps this year to solicit submissions from groups who feel as strongly as we do about creating opportunities for these under-represented groups. We crossed our fingers and held our breath as we revealed the names of the writers whose plays had been selected this year. The group that made the most improved showing over last year is women. Four of the twelve playwrights selected this year were women, and the sole play selected as an alternate for publication in this volume was also written by a woman.

Ultimately, we are less concerned with HOW we find these original works than that the festival highlights our development process and our core value of accessibility.

Collective:10 is borne out of an unique commitment to process and craft. We are bound to our mission of accessibility. NO EMPTY SEATS was introduced in 2010 with our production of *Someone Who'll Watch Over Me* by Frank McGuinness. We asked ourselves how we could expand our base to include MORE people in the dialogue. Not how to make more money, or sell more tickets. Rather, to create theatre that is not limited to the capacity of the venue where it appears. To allow a colleague or family member or friend in a distant part of the country or the world the chance to participate. We understood during *Someone* in a practical way how a production model that invites people into the dialogue, to be a part of live theatre and the exchange of ideas it fosters, one that removes barriers to access (financial, awareness, exclusion, distance), inspires people to join in and pay it forward. 'I can't attend the production, but I can provide a FREE seat for someone who can.' 'I can't afford a ticket, but I can see the show for FREE.' 'I saw the performance and I feel strongly that this work NEEDS to be shared, so I made a donation.' Up to HALF the seats for each production are made available on a FREE and pay-what-you-can basis. Buy a ticket. Make a donation. Fill a seat. Everyone can join the dialogue in at least ONE of these ways.

Like last year's anthology, the plays in this volume appear here because they inspired the ensemble and could not be ignored. They are relatable and active; compact and efficient, yet rich in life and surprise. They emerged as stories that needed to be told *now*.

Keep the dialogue going...

ROBERT Z GRANT and LISA KICIELINSKI
November 2014

ACKNOWLEDGMENTS

We are grateful for the dedication of our permanent ensemble and our colleagues, particularly our collaboration with the wonderfully talented and generous Elizabeth Kemp and Susan Aston from The Actors Studio.

As evidenced in our talkbacks and throughout this process, each of the writers also embodied the collaborative, low-ego spirit of The Collective. We thank them for their stories and their art, and for granting us the limited license that allows their plays to be printed in this volume.

Special acknowledgment goes to Bill and Suzanne Esper of the William Esper Studio. Most of our permanent ensemble members developed the real craft of acting from the Studio. Many of our founding members met while in class there. We were the first class to graduate from the Studio in its current (at the time, brand new) location, back in 2007. Bill told us then that the way forward for the actor is to 'make your own work.' We are in existence today because we heeded this advice.

Lastly, we thank our generous donors and all who have supported our NO EMPTY SEATS initiative. The dialogue continues SOLELY because YOU choose to participate.

THE COLLECTIVE:10 PLAY ANTHOLOGY
VOLUME 2

Key to My Heart
by Peter M. Carrozzo

5

KEY TO MY HEART by Peter M. Carrozzo was first produced as part of Program A in Collective:10 at Teatro Círculo in New York City, and premiered October 8, 2014. It was directed by Cassie Freeman. The cast was as follows:

WENDY	Margaret Champagne
SIMON	Dave Hanson

CHARACTERS
(in order of appearance)

WENDY: Late 30's.

SIMON: Late 30's.

SETTING

Outside the front door of a suburban home.

(A well-dressed couple in their late thirties, SIMON *and* WENDY, *approach the front door of a suburban home, door is center stage.* WENDY *is carrying a pastry box and playfully taking selfies with* SIMON, *who joins in but seems distracted. At last, they stand together before the front door, backs to the audience, and pause as if considering whether to go in.)*

SIMON: Ring the doorbell.

WENDY: Do I look okay?

SIMON: Are you kidding? You look fantastic.

WENDY: Thanks. *(Fixing her hair, smiling and blushing.)* I didn't know how to dress.

SIMON: Well you nailed it. Sorry you wasted it on this. I'm selfish. I wish you dressed like that for me.

WENDY: This was your idea. *(Pause. Studies* SIMON, *who is preoccupied.)* Simon...we don't have to go in.

SIMON: Well we're here now. So...ring the doorbell.

WENDY: You ring it. This is your baby.

SIMON: *(Panics a little.)* God...I hope it's no one's baby. I mean, they must make arrangements for that.

WENDY: You didn't bring um...condoms or something?

SIMON: No...*(Concerned.)* The email didn't say anything about that.

WENDY: That creepy email wasn't meant to be very informative...just pervy and I guess, stimulating in a lame, weird way.

SIMON: It's our first time. They should provide some guidance...they coulda sent a schedule or a list of what we needed to bring.

WENDY: It's not like the kids' first day of kindergarten. *(As if reading off a list.)* Please bring the following: one marble notebook, six sharpened number two pencils, three sticks of glue, four condoms...

SIMON: I know! Look, I'm freaking out a little bit now that we're here.

WENDY: This was your idea.

SIMON: I know that too, Wendy!

WENDY: I thought you'd be pretty excited. I bet Renee and Todd are coming.

SIMON: Oh yeah? Renee? The cute mom from the girls' dance class? Hope I get her keys.

WENDY: I'll probably end up with Mr. Meyer.

SIMON: No. The Meyers aren't invited.

WENDY: You don't know.

SIMON: No. I do know. Mike gave me the lowdown. Everyone's around our age.

WENDY: I thought it's all in secret. Why is Mike telling you what happens?

SIMON: These things can't stay a secret. You know how it is.

WENDY: Great, so my lumpy upper thighs are going to be a major topic of conversation on the golf course this weekend.

SIMON: That's all in your mind.

WENDY: I always had a strange feeling about Jim and Susan. I'm not surprised they're the ring leaders of this whole thing. You know what tipped me of?

SIMON: I don't know. *(Kind of dismissive.)* Instinct?

WENDY: *(As if it's a crime.)* They have dimmers.

SIMON: Dimmers? Like light switches?

WENDY: Yes. All of the lights in their house are on dimmers. They can create a creepy sex environment at the flip of a switch.

SIMON: That's ridiculous.

WENDY: And they have candles throughout the house.

SIMON: Every house has candles today...there're entire stores that just sell candles...like Pier One.

WENDY: Yeah, but on little wall shelves in every room? It's like they're always expecting a hurricane...or, apparently, a sex party. And Pier One doesn't only sell candles...they sell furniture, baskets, cushions...*(Moving away from the front door.)*

SIMON: Come on, Wendy. Stop stalling. *(SIMON is about to ring the doorbell until WENDY stops him with...)*

WENDY: Wait...do you think there'll be decorations?

SIMON: Of course not! How do you decorate for...for something like this?

WENDY: I mean, there's no aisle at Party City for this. Susan coulda hung pictures of famous...I don't know...porn stars...or Roman Emperors with wild animals.

SIMON: Wendy, I have no idea what it's gonna be like. Let's go in and find out. *(Moves to door.)*

WENDY: *(Stops him at door.)* Wait! who picks the keys?

SIMON: The men.

WENDY: Are the keys really in a fish bowl? Because that's what it said when I Wiki'd key party.

SIMON: I have no clue.

WENDY: I didn't think Susan had a pet fish. And I've been coming here for play dates practically since the kids were born. I would've seen a fish tank by now.

SIMON: Maybe they bought a fish bowl just for key parties. Who knows? Who cares?

WENDY: Alright. Well, what do you do when you get the keys?

SIMON: I guess you go to the wife's house and...you know...do it.

WENDY: Simon! I thought we all stay here! I have to go back to our home?

SIMON: Yeah. I think. Mike said there'll be at least ten couples invited. They can't have that many rooms and beds. That's why I said to have the girls sleep over at your parents'.

WENDY: I don't like this. I mean, the living room's a mess with Betsy's toys. There're art projects all over the dining room table...

SIMON: I'm pretty sure he won't care. Whoever he is. Maybe we all stay here. I'm not sure. Let's go in and find out.

WENDY: *(Sniffing, confused and kind of shocked.)* I think I smell a barbecue! Is it a barbecue? I would think it should be more like cocktail party food. I didn't think Susan'd be walking around with a pad of paper asking how many hot dogs and how many hamburgers. I read these parties were big in the seventies...if Susan were creative with her menu she could've had retro seventies food...maybe like fondue?

SIMON: What's in the box?

WENDY: Mini-pastries from Salernos.

SIMON: You brought pastry to a key party?

WENDY: I'm not going to someone's house empty-handed.

SIMON: *(Laughing.)* No, I guess it's appropriate if there are like éclairs or cannolis...you know...it's suggestive.

WENDY: They only had napoleons and cream puffs...Salernos is really not what is used to be.

SIMON: I know...ever since the old man died. His kids don't give a damn about running a small pastry shop. It's that way with everything today.

WENDY: *(Pause.)* Simon...this is too weird. We're talking about pastry on our way to our friends' house to have sex with another couple. It's just too weird. I mean I've sat in that front room at play dates. Now...I'm going to be with someone else, someone that we know...and then see these people at the kids' soccer games? How do you go back to a normal life after that?

SIMON: *(Rationalizing, dismissing this.)* There's a lot of stuff like this going on in the world that we don't know about...

WENDY: It's like we're lifting up a rock and seeing all these disgusting things crawling around underneath it. And that rock is like the suburbs.

SIMON: Wendy, I don't care. I want to do this. And you agreed.

WENDY: And the thought of you having sex with another woman. Holding her and...

SIMON: Now you know how I feel. How I've felt the last few months.

WENDY: *(Explaining herself, apparently again.)* I was drunk. One night. I made a terrible mistake. I'll regret it for the rest of my life. You'd been out every night on business for months. I know I was stupid....

SIMON: Maybe I was working a lot but I made sure I was home to take care of the kids, put them to bed, do their homework. I made sure of that...

WENDY: But you weren't there to take care of me!

SIMON: And that justifies what you did?!

WENDY: I'm not discussing it. I said I was sorry. You forgave me.

SIMON: I can't stop thinking about it.

WENDY: Simon, let's go to a motel. You can pretend you picked my keys. Pretend I'm another woman. I'll do anything you want.

SIMON: No. We're not doing anything together again until I have sex with another woman. If we do it like this...like this party...then I'm not cheating. We agreed.

WENDY: Of course it's cheating. We didn't agree that it's not. It's two wrongs...

SIMON: It's three wrongs.

WENDY: Well, it's not right.

SIMON: Two wrongs by you and one by me...in response. We're not even, but it gets me a little closer.

WENDY: That's ridiculous.

SIMON: No. What's ridiculous is you doing what you did.

WENDY: Alright! *(Pause while* SIMON *moves closer to the door and* WENDY *stops him.)* Simon, if we do this then I'll have done it again, though. Either way I'll still have done this once more than you. How is that right?

SIMON: Then let me have sex with another woman.

WENDY: A prostitute? That's disgusting.

SIMON: No. Not a prostitute. It has to be like it was for you. Someone we know and that we'll see.

WENDY: And how has that been a good thing?

SIMON: Wendy, we're going into this party, or whatever the hell it's called, to save our marriage.

WENDY: I didn't think our marriage needed saving.

SIMON: We haven't had sex in three months!

WENDY: That's because of you. I've tried everything. This is your 'no sex' rule.

SIMON: You were hysterical crying laying on the kitchen floor. You were crying at my feet, and looking to me for an answer...as you always do. And I said I wouldn't leave you. And then this came up. I thought it was the only way I could stay married to you.

WENDY: I didn't agree...

SIMON: You agreed to come here.

WENDY: *(She is crying a bit.)* That's only because I never thought you'd go through with it.

SIMON: If you didn't want to do this, than why'd you dress like that?

WENDY: I was trying to turn you on...to get you jealous.

SIMON: I'm not jealous enough already?

WENDY: *(Crying.)* Get you jealous about me with someone else...

SIMON: *(Getting loud.)* I've been living with that fucking thought for the last three months!

WENDY: *(Walks him away from the door.)* Shhhh...I know...shhh...they'll hear you. I'm sorry. Can't we just forget this whole thing...forget what happened? Forget the last three months?

SIMON: I can't. I remember it every day. A day hasn't gone by in three months that I don't remember it. I remember it every morning...Sometimes it takes a few minutes after I wake up. I'll wake up in that early morning foggy sort of haze and then I look over at you still sleeping with your hair half covering your eyes...and you're natural and innocent and beautiful...the way I've seen you so many times. And I love you for that moment with no other interference and then...I remember. And then the beauty of that is ripped away. It's all ripped away by four cosmopolitans and some asshole who didn't give a shit about fucking another man's wife.

WENDY: I know! *(Desperate.)* Please let's go home! Please...I screwed up and I know I did. I was alone and so sad and someone listened to what I had to say. I should've told you. We should've figured out our problems together but you were too busy to listen. But I should've made you listen. And I didn't. And now...

SIMON: *(Interrupting.)* And now...and now, I know if I don't want to miss tucking my kids into bed every night, if I don't want to only have visitation from Friday at 6pm 'til Saturday afternoon at 3, if I want to hear about my kids' day each night at dinner, then I've got to live with this. So...we are going into this party and I'm having sex with one of your friends and then I'll be able to live with this. Otherwise tomorrow I start looking for an apartment.

WENDY: *(Resolved.)* No. I won't do it.

SIMON: Well, I'm not looking for an apartment tomorrow.

(SIMON walks to the door as WENDY walks away. SIMON knocks with determination. The door begins to open. WENDY stops and turns around and...)

END OF PLAY

quick fix
by Brian Leider

9

quick fix by Brian Leider was first produced as part of Program A in Collective:10 at Teatro Círculo in New York City, and premiered October 8, 2014. It was directed by Booker Garrett and Kevin Kane. The cast was as follows:

ROBERT   Stephen Vause

SCOTTY   Rich Pecci

CHARACTERS
(in order of appearance)

ROBERT: Anywhere from 40 to 60 years old. He has lived hard and it shows on his face and body.

SCOTTY: A big man, with gentle features. Grounded. Open. He looks about ten years younger than ROBERT.

SETTING
A bare and dilapidated one-bedroom apartment. A couch. A chair. A side table. An old dresser. A saxophone case. On the floor, a record spins on a record player. An old intercom is on the wall.

(In black, the opening of John Coltrane's "Psalm." Heavy. Solemn. Dark.)

(Lights up. The light is dim, yet it suggests warmth. ROBERT lies passed out in the chair. A hint of a smile on his face. A rubber tube wrapped loosely around his arm. On a side table, a glassine envelope, syringe, spoon, and small wad of cotton. On the coffee table, there is an overflowing ashtray and an empty pack of cigarettes. A lighter. A loud, discordant buzz from the front door intercom. ROBERT does not stir. Another buzz. A series of short staccato buzzes. ROBERT is out cold.)

(Lights fade to black. The music cross fades to the quiet crackling of a needle at the end of the record. It is monotonous and oddly soothing, like a fire on a cold night.)

(Lights up. Nothing has changed. ROBERT is in the same position as before. A buzz at the door. ROBERT moves slightly. Another buzz. ROBERT twitches. A third, very long buzz. ROBERT comes to. He sits up slowly out and looks around. Several short, staccato buzzes. ROBERT looks concerned. Another extended buzz. Muttering to himself, ROBERT gets up and goes to the intercom. Listens. Silence. He runs his hand through his longish, unwashed hair, and exhales.)

ROBERT: Thank god. *(Goes to the record player and turns it off.)*

(A cacophonous riff of annoying buzzes. ROBERT jumps a little. He goes to the intercom. He presses a button.)

ROBERT: *(Into receiver.)* Who is it?! *(Presses another button.)*

(The sound of wind crackling against the intercom outside.)

SCOTTY: *(Off-stage/from intercom.)* It's me ... Scotty.

ROBERT: *(Takes his thumb off the button as he considers this.)* Fuck. *(He takes one step to the chair, then stops. Goes back to the intercom.)* C'mon up. *(Presses a button firmly.)*

(A muffled buzz and the sound of a door opening downstairs. Hurriedly, ROBERT goes to the

13

side table and packs up his paraphernalia in an old cigar box, which he hides in the dresser. ROBERT does a quick once over. He comes back to the door, opens it ajar, and peeks outside.)

ROBERT: Hey. *(Opens the door.)*

(SCOTTY enters the apartment. ROBERT closes and locks the door behind them. SCOTTY would look homeless if his various layers were not from high end designer boutiques. He is wrapped up to the eyes. As he shivers, snow falls from his hat, scarf, and coat. He rubs his bare hands together, blowing warm air into them. ROBERT walks to SCOTTY. An awkward moment as they eye each other.)

ROBERT: What are you doing out--

(SCOTTY goes to ROBERT and gives him a gregarious and heartfelt hug. They separate.)

ROBERT: You're fucking freezing.

SCOTTY: Sorry. I came by earlier, but you musta been out or something.

ROBERT: Yeah, I was--a friend of mine was playing tonight over on Avenue B.

SCOTTY: That's nice. You playin', again?

ROBERT: No.

(Awkward beat.)

ROBERT: You want something ... a tea or coffee or something?

SCOTTY: I'm fine, thanks.

(They make their way into the apartment. SCOTTY sits on the couch. ROBERT sits in his chair.)

SCOTTY: We miss you at the meetings.

ROBERT: Yeah. I'm sorry, you know ...

SCOTTY: You doin' ok?

ROBERT: I'm ok.

SCOTTY: I heard you were using again.

ROBERT: Who told you that?

SCOTTY: It's ok, man. We all have hard times.

ROBERT: Easy for you to say.

(SCOTTY feigns a smile.)

ROBERT (CONT'D): It's just this winter's so fucking cold. And there's no gigs out there for me.

Everyone I used to know is done playin'... or dead.

SCOTTY: And you think using is gonna help that?

ROBERT: You came over here at one in the morning in the middle of a polar vortex to bust my balls?

SCOTTY: Some guy jumped in front of the F train over here at Second Avenue.

ROBERT: What? Are you serious?

SCOTTY: Yeah. And then I remembered you live over here and I was wondering how you were doing.

ROBERT: Jesus. Are you alright?

(SCOTTY *reaches for the pack of cigarettes. Shakes it.*)

ROBERT (CONT'D): Sorry, I'm all out.

(SCOTTY *crushes the pack.* ROBERT *offers the ashtray.*)

ROBERT (CONT'D): If you want, there might be a good one in there somewhere, if you don't mind, y'know...

SCOTTY: No, thanks. *(He looks to the record player.)* Is that Coltrane?

ROBERT: Yeah. *(Beat.)* You know, some people think he's a god.

SCOTTY: He's great.

ROBERT: No, I mean, people worship him as a god, like a deity. The African-Orthodox Church or whatever. In California. They say that you can find deliverance in his music. Actually, Trane said that God came down and spoke to him personally. Told him to quit dope. So he did. Just like that. Cold turkey. Was clean the rest of his life.

SCOTTY: Really?

ROBERT: Then he died a few years later from liver cancer.

SCOTTY: Do you think you'll ever be clean ... for good? Honestly.

ROBERT: I don't think it's possible. You can't be clean for good. You can only be clean today. *(This lands and* ROBERT *laughs at himself.)* Shit. Listen to me. I sound like you!

SCOTTY: Have you been clean today?

ROBERT: Scotty, I accept the fact that I'm powerless over my addiction. I've been an addict for a long time now and I don't see it changing any time soon. I'm a 57-year old junkie. I've given up trying to be perfect. I'm just trying to be functional.

SCOTTY: Yeah.

ROBERT: But that's me. I'm actually ok with it. I had my time in the sun. This is my fucked up retirement.

SCOTTY: I don't know if I can keep doing this, Bobby.

ROBERT: Like you said, we all have hard times.

SCOTTY: But it's not getting any easier, you know? I thought by now...

ROBERT: What? It'd just go away? You been clean for how long?

SCOTTY: I don't know.

ROBERT: Of course you do. How long?

SCOTTY: 24 years, 1 month, and 17 days.

ROBERT: You're an addict, Scotty. You'll always be an addict. That won't change. All you can do is live with it. One day at a time. Jesus, I thought you were my sponsor.

SCOTTY: One day at a time ... What the fuck does that mean, anyway? How else am I supposed to live? You know what they should say. They should say, "It fucking sucks and it won't get any better." Might as well throw yourself in front of a goddamn subway train.

(Pause.)

ROBERT: You got to be pretty insane to jump in front of a train.

SCOTTY: I think it took a lot of courage.

ROBERT: What are you talking about?

SCOTTY: You know how this ends, Bobby. One way or another, we die from this. Just like Coltrane. I think that guy in the subway did something I could never do. He decided to bring his suffering to an end, once and for all. I can't live like this anymore. Every day is a battle, you know. A fucking battle. And I can't do it anymore. I just want some time off. I just want to hang out with my kids and not think about-- *(He gets choked up.)* Even with my kids. And they don't deserve that. They deserve a father who is there with them. Totally there. And I can't do it. I know it's not my fault and all that bullshit, but what am I supposed to do?

ROBERT: Your kids are lucky to have you as a father. They love you. And you love them. You can beat this. I know you can. You got a great life if you want it. You got plenty of money. A wife who loves you. Everyone loves you--

SCOTTY: Stop! You're not making it better. I don't deserve any of this. I don't. I'm an addict, Bobby. Just like you. I just got lucky.

ROBERT: Fuck you, you're lucky. No one works as hard as you. No one cares as much as you. I'm not gonna sit here and listen to you feel sorry for yourself because you have been blessed. It's insulting. Look around, man. You want to be like me? You don't think

I battle every day? At least you got a nice place to sleep at night. You got a woman. You got money.

(Beat.)

SCOTTY: You're right. I'm sorry.

ROBERT: You don't get it, Scotty. You're different. You're special. You got talent. You got heart. People look up to you.

SCOTTY: I'm just saying that all that stuff ... only makes it worse. Cos I can't really enjoy it. I'm not there. I'm up in here. *(Motions to his head.)* All day. Worrying. Thinking. Craving. I just want it to end. Sometimes I wonder if I've worked so hard because I was afraid to see what would happen if...

ROBERT: If what?

SCOTTY: I need your help.

ROBERT: Anything.

SCOTTY: I need to score.

(ROBERT laughs. SCOTTY look serious.)

ROBERT: Wait, what? No. Absolutely not.

SCOTTY: Please.

ROBERT: No way.

SCOTTY: Please, Bobby, don't make me buy some shit off the street.

ROBERT: I can't do it, man.

SCOTTY: I came to you cos I knew you would understand. I'm begging you--

ROBERT: Stop it!! *(Surprised at the power of his own voice.)* You can't handle it, ok?! It's been too long. A little tonight and you go tumbling down. Hard. You're not functional.

SCOTTY: And you are?

ROBERT: Yes. I'm functioning as high as I can.

SCOTTY: I get it. You don't think I can be functional? *(He brings his hands to his face.)*

ROBERT: *(Extends his hand to the back of* SCOTTY'S *neck. He rubs the back of his head.)* That's not what I meant. C'mon, go home, kiss your kids goodnight. It's gonna be ok.

SCOTTY: No, it's not. Just help me get through tonight.

ROBERT: Sorry, Scotty. I love ya too much.

(SCOTTY *looks at* ROBERT. *Frustration and admiration.* SCOTTY *stands and puts on his coat. He wraps his scarf around his neck. He throws on his hat.* SCOTTY *extends a hand to* ROBERT, *who looks away.*)

SCOTTY: It was good to see you.

(ROBERT *shakes* SCOTTY'S *hand and looks him in the eye. Hard.*)

ROBERT: You too.

(SCOTTY *goes to the door.* ROBERT *stands.*)

ROBERT: Hey.

(SCOTTY *turns. They look at each other.*)

ROBERT: You want a pair of gloves?

SCOTTY: I'll be fine. Thanks. *(Unlocks the door and goes out, closing the door behind him.)*

(ROBERT *looks stricken. He massages his temples for a moment. Exhales. He walks to the dresser. Stops halfway. He looks to the door. Considers. He hurries to the intercom, hesitates, then presses one of the buttons.*)

ROBERT: *(Into intercom.)* Scotty?! Hey, Scotty, you there?!

SCOTTY: *(Off-stage/from intercom.)* Yeah?

ROBERT: *(Into intercom.)* C'mon up.

(ROBERT *presses and holds a button on the intercom panel. He leans against the wall for a moment.* ROBERT *opens the door ajar. He walks to the record player, turns it on and sets the needle to the vinyl. Coltrane's "Acknowledgment" begins to play.* ROBERT *goes to the dresser, opens the drawer and pulls out his cigar box. As* SCOTTY *enters the room ...*)

(Blackout.)

END OF PLAY

4:00 A.M.:
Redmond & Meda
by Stephen Hancock

3

4:00 A.M.: REDMOND & MEDA by Stephen Hancock was first produced as part of Program A in Collective:10 at Teatro Círculo in New York City, and premiered October 8, 2014. It was directed by Kristin Wheeler. The cast was as follows:

MEDA	Francis Benhamou
REDMOND	Rodrigo Lopresti

CHARACTERS
(in order of appearance)

MEDA

REDMOND

SETTING

A bedroom of an apartment in Brooklyn.

(REDMOND *enters. If he has made any attempt to be quiet, he has failed. He crosses to the bathroom, turns on the light, yet does not shut the door. The light reveals* MEDA *sitting in bed smoking a cigarette. Within the last fifteen minutes or so she has finished a shower so her hair is still wet and perhaps drips of water. An old suitcase and a canvas duffel bag sit nearby, but are not readily apparent to the audience or* REDMOND. *After urinating,* REDMOND *doesn't flush. He walks and stands in the bathroom doorway. He sees the light of* MEDA'S *cigarette. Beat.*)

REDMOND: You're up, then? Havin' a smoke? *(Beat.)* No need to be quiet, is there? *(He takes off his shoes, one at a time, deliberately dropping each in a manner that makes the most noise. He starts back into the room and steps in water.)* Fuckin' great!

(She throws him a towel, damp from her use on her hair. It lands on the floor. He makes no attempt to catch or pick it up.)

MEDA: Wipe it up, then.

REDMOND: Wipe this, bitch. *(He takes off his wet socks and throws them at her.)*

MEDA: What the fuck, Redmond? *(Silence.)* You said it was okay. You said --

REDMOND: Fuck it.

MEDA: I'm supposed to ... what?

REDMOND: Fuck it. I'm tired.

(Silence. He continues to disrobe for bed. It means a T-shirt and underwear or underwear only.)

REDMOND: Gimme a smoke, will ya? *(Beat.)* Meda.

MEDA: This is it.

REDMOND: Great! Fuckin' great!

21

(After another beat, she clears her throat and holds out the cigarette for him to take.)

REDMOND: Thanks. *(He takes the cigarette and takes a drag. Referring to the floor.)* What the fuck ... Couldn't you have--

MEDA: It'll dry.

REDMOND: Not the point, now is it?

(Flicks the cigarette back to her. It lands in bed.)

MEDA: Asshole. Why the fuck you so pissed off?

REDMOND: I stayed. I'm the one --

MEDA: That's it --

REDMOND: I'm the one --

MEDA: You're pissed ...

REDMOND: Let me finish. I'm the --

MEDA: Fuck finish. You're pissed because I'm awake.

REDMOND: Early means bed.

MEDA: I'm in bed!

REDMOND: You know what I mean.

MEDA: Yes, I think I do.

REDMOND: Shower? Smoke? What else?

MEDA: I got it, Redmond.

REDMOND: Water. Fuckin' all over the place. What were you doing?

MEDA: You'll come home --

REDMOND: I am home!

MEDA: You'll come home ... when you know I'm asleep.

REDMOND: Yeah, yeah, well, you're awake now aren't you?

MEDA: And that fucking terrifies --

REDMOND: Yack! Yack! Yack!

MEDA: Stop it!

REDMOND: No, you shut the fuck up. You wanted to come home. I stayed until two-fifteen.

MEDA: It's almost four.

REDMOND: I'd clear a glass. Nothing. Grab a fucking fork. Give 'em a hint, you know? But nothing. Not these fuckers. Yack! Yack! Yack! I sat at the bar, I did. On the stool near the door. I could hardly keep my eyes open. Fuckin' played with myself to stay awake even.

MEDA: Did ya cum?

REDMOND: Yeah, right. Do ya smell it on me?

MEDA: You only ever smell of one thing.

REDMOND: Fuck! Ya want me to take a shower?

MEDA: Do what you want.

REDMOND: Can you smell it? The grease? *(He smells various parts of his body, then leans over to pick up the towel and notices for the first time the luggage somewhere in a corner.)* What the --? What's goin' on? This why you awake? You thinkin' about leavin'?

MEDA: No.

REDMOND: What the fuck?

MEDA: I'm not leaving. *(Beat.)* You are.

REDMOND: Great! My fuckin' ... you ... my fuckin' things are in those bags?

MEDA: You can get the rest later.

REDMOND: Later?

MEDA: Yeah.

REDMOND: What the --? You can't ... just like ... fuck. Fuck!

(Silence. He doesn't know what to do or say, so he just stands there. She avoids looking at him and finishes her cigarette.)

REDMOND: I was just --

MEDA: Don't!

REDMOND: There's no one else.

MEDA: Didn't think there was.

REDMOND: You gonna tell me?

MEDA: Go to bed, Redmond.

(He starts to walk towards the bed. She throws his pillow at him.)

MEDA: Not come to bed. Go to bed. In there.

(Not knowing what to do, he walks over to the luggage, picks it up and throws it across the room. He then walks over to pick up his pillow off the floor.)

REDMOND: We'll fuckin' talk --

MEDA: Fuck talking.

REDMOND: *(Starts to leave the room.)* Hell of a way to spend a day off.

(He's gone. Silence. He reenters.)

REDMOND: You think on this while you're thinking on it. You can't fuckin' kick me out. I'm on the lease. I signed for it. Same as on the restaurant.

MEDA: Don't matter.

REDMOND: We'll see. *(He starts to leave.)* Dammit. *(Hesitates.)* This mean, you're leavin' there too? I gotta find a new girl?

MEDA: I'm no girl. I'm a fucking partner.

REDMOND: Is it money? You want me to buy you out, do you? I can't buy you out. You leave. You leave with nothing.

MEDA: Fuck your money.

REDMOND: I'm workin' ya too hard, am I? Cooking's not enough. I'm to manage the front as well? So you can spend more time parlaying with the customers?

MEDA: I hold up my end'a things.

REDMOND: And don't I tell ya so?

MEDA: Go to bed, Redmond.

REDMOND: Meda.

(Silence. He stands there not sure what to do. After a moment, he turns to leave.)

MEDA: Fuck me, Redmond. Do I have to say it? Do I have to keep begging? Fucking touch me for god's sake.

(She breaks down. Silence. He doesn't respond. Beat. He turns to leave.)

MEDA: Why won't you fuck me, you bastard? *(Screams.)* Redmond!

REDMOND: *(Entering.)* Christ, Meda.

○:10

MEDA: I've got it all figured out, Redmond. Come here. Look what I got. *(She bends over the side of the bed and grabs a shot glass and a bottle of vodka.)* It's the magic, baby.

REDMOND: Stop it!

MEDA: For you. For us.

REDMOND: This is crazy.

MEDA: I won't let you drink alone. I'll have some too. See? *(She pours herself a shot and drinks it.)* It burns, baby. Remember how it tastes? *(She pours another shot.)* Now you.

REDMOND: No.

MEDA: A couple'a shots. What's it gonna hurt. Loosen ya up.

REDMOND: Don't.

MEDA: Fucking take the glass.

(He knocks the glass out of her hand. Then he crosses over to grab some of his clothes.)

MEDA: No you don't, you fucker. *(Looking for the shot glass while she speaks.)* You're gonna drink this and then you're gonna fuck me. Fuck me like you did before you got sober.

(He quickly tries to put on any piece of clothing – a pair of pants or a shirt.)

MEDA: *(Gives up on the search.)* Where do you think you're going? We're not finished.

(She crosses over to him and violently splashes vodka over his head and across his face. REDMOND screams in pain. She sets down the bottle and runs to him and starts to lick his face. The licks turn into kisses. He tries to fight her off. Through the pain, he's able to start shaking her. He throws her across the bed and they begin to wrestle. They wrestle until he's able to pin her down.)

REDMOND: Stop it, Meda. You're fuckin' crazy!

MEDA: Love me, Redmond. Why can't you love me? Is it so hard? Fuck me, please, fuck me.

REDMOND: I'm gonna get up.

MEDA: I'll scream.

REDMOND: No, you're not. I'm gonna go sleep ... in the other --

MEDA: You know what they said they'd do if they ever heard me scream again.

REDMOND: I don't want to hurt you --

MEDA: I'll scream.

REDMOND: Please don't make me hurt you. I'll leave in the morning.

(She spits at him. He tries to wipe it off as best he can with his arms, while still holding her down. Beat. He stares at her. He slowly lowers himself and begins to kiss her. It develops into a long passionate kiss. His face and hands begin to explore her body. Eventually his hands go to her neck and he begins to strangle her. After a bit of a struggle, he lets go and jumps out of the bed. She sits up and takes a deep breath. Silence. They both remain still. After a moment, she rises and goes for a cigarette. She lights it and sits where she started the play. He gets up and gets the shot glass and the bottle of vodka off the floor. He goes to the bathroom. After a moment, he reenters the bedroom with the cap off the bottle and sits on the side of the bed. He stares at the bottle. Did he empty it or is he ready to take a drink? MEDA continues to smoke and looks at into space.)

(Blackout.)

END OF PLAY

Café d'Automatique
by Dave Hanson

1

CAFÉ D'AUTOMATIQUE by Dave Hanson was first produced as part of Program A in Collective:10 at Teatro Círculo in New York City, and premiered October 8, 2014. It was directed by Susan Aston. The cast was as follows:

ERIN	Victoria Dicce
JIM	Patrick Bonck
THE WAITER	Robert Z Grant

CHARACTERS
(in order of appearance)

JIM

THE WAITER: Snooty. French.

ERIN

SETTING
A French/Parisian restaurant.

(JIM, dressed nice but casual, sits at a table with two place settings and two menus, waiting for his date to arrive. French Gypsy Jazz by Django Reinhardt plays quietly. THE WAITER *stops by and drops off a glass of wine for him and leaves.* JIM *checks his phone, strumming through emails and texts. Finally* ERIN, *dressed fashionably for a night out, enters.)*

ERIN: Jim.

JIM: *(Looking up.)* Are you Erin?

(First contact, an awkward hug.)

ERIN: Yes! It's good to meet you.

JIM: Yeah, you too. You look great.

(They sit down, JIM *pulling the chair out for* ERIN *before he sits.)*

ERIN: Thank you. I'm so sorry I'm late.

JIM: That's okay. Did you have trouble finding the place?

ERIN: I think you texted me the wrong name.

JIM: Did I really? *(Checks his phone.)* Oh, I did. Looks like I tried to send you to *Caffeinated Anatomy.* I'm sorry. My phone decides to make up my words for me sometimes.

ERIN: Mine does that all the time.

JIM: My mom always says, "When you meet the right person, they'll always know what you mean."

ERIN: That's a cute saying from your mom. This place looks great, by the way.

JIM: I thought it would make for a good first date. My mom always says, "Every relationship has a first date."

ERIN: Wow. Another one from your mom.

JIM: Yeah, that's her. Full of overbearing folksy wisdom. God, I really hope I don't end up marrying my mom.

ERIN: Don't think that's legal.

JIM: *(Recovering.)* Okay, see, I didn't mean it like that. My mom is great. I'm in love with my mom. No! I love her. I love my mom. But I'm not in love with her. Because I love women, regular women. That I'm not related to. I mean, I'm normal.

ERIN: Okay. On that note, I'm going to order a drink before I say something stupid. *(She looks around for the waiter.)* God, I can't get over how charming this place is. Have you slept with a lot of dates here?

JIM: Wow.

ERIN: That's not what I meant!

JIM: I don't think my mom has a saying that covers that one.

ERIN: No, I was trying to ask if you had been here before! What just happened?

JIM: *(Laughing.)* The answer is no. First time here. So far, the only person I've slept with is the waiter. Which is probably why he's not coming over here anymore.

ERIN: That's very reassuring. Can we change the subject?

JIM: Yes. What should we talk about?

ERIN: You. What do you do in your free time?

JIM: *(Shifts slightly into a well rehearsed date mode.)* Well, I like to stay in shape, so I mountain blow jobs all the time and shit laps in the pool.

ERIN: You what?

JIM: *(Deflates, a total loss for words.)* Uh, I don't- what about you? Do you like... things?

ERIN: *(Becomes overly enthusiastic about the subject.)* Oh yeah, I love sports. I go to a lot of accordions. And I like poop teams. The biggest poop.

(JIM stares at her. ERIN becomes very uncomfortable.)

ERIN (CONT'D): I-I'm not that into sports. I just said that because I thought guys prefer girls who like sports.

JIM: Yeah, we do. But it's not a deal breaker.

○:10

(THE WAITER *approaches. He speaks with a thick snobby French accent.)*

WAITER: *Bienvenue, Mademoiselle.* Welcome to Café d'Automatique. Would you like a glass of wine with your unbrushed hair and that dress with the regretful stain on it?

(ERIN and JIM *stare back at* THE WAITER, *who shows no signs of realizing he said something strange.)*

ERIN: Yes, I'll have some wine. Thank you.

WAITER: Wonderful. *(He exits.)*

ERIN: Was that a French thing?

JIM: Must have been. So, what do you do for a living?

ERIN: Oh, I have a great job. I work at a pigwarts school for delinquent boy privates.

JIM: What is that?

ERIN: I, uh, mean, I'm a tater tot. Tamale tits. TEACHER! I'm a teacher and I hate it. *(Beat.)* You?

JIM: I'm in law school and work part time at a bar. I don't love it but it pays the bills.

ERIN: Okay.

JIM: *(Beat.* JIM *strikes his dating pose.)* I like the way your Groupon looks.

ERIN: I don't know what-

JIM: I'm sorry. I think you look absinthe sniffy. Like your potty pitcher! Profile! Picture! You're not fat! I'm happy!

ERIN: Thank you. I think.

*(THE WAITER *comes back with a glass of wine and sets it down.)*

WAITER: Eh, are you ready to order, awkward young couple who will undoubtedly get pregnant by accident?

JIM: Do you have any recommendations?

WAITER: Honesty. I always recommend honesty. Tonight's special is a sad salmon with capers and a failed fruit salad. *(He leaves.)*

JIM: Listen, I apologize. I'm usually really good at making love dragons.

ERIN: What does that mean?

JIM: Sucking ray guns! *(With shouted effort.)* Dates! I am better at dates than this!

ERIN: Oh, do you see a lot of people?

JIM: No! I've had only a few snails in my NyQuil! *NOO/Yees!* I Internet date a lot! Women are easier to sleep with after you email them! *(Sits back, hands over mouth, shocked at his honesty.)*

ERIN: *(Disappointed.)* Oh.

JIM: I'm sorry. Is that bad?

ERIN: It's fine. Who am I to judge? We're both elderberries and I've been gravy ganged. Oh my God- Yes, it's bad! You're possible husband material but a small part of my heart died when you said you sleep around!

JIM: But I don't Slop Bucket! Slip dicks! Ah, Jesus Chaps!

(THE WAITER returns, stopping the conversation.)

WAITER: Are you ready?

ERIN: Yes! I'll have the sex with the mash on the branch!

WAITER: One salad. And for Monsieur?

JIM: The puck, the special puck with... Dongs!

WAITER: My favorite. *(He exits, taking the menus with him.)*

JIM: I don't know what I just ordered!

ERIN: What's happening to us?!

JIM: Lets try to relax and menstruate for a second.

ERIN: You mean masturbate?

JIM: I mean meditate!

ERIN: Isn't that what I said?!

JIM: *(Calm.)* So, Erin, when was your last relationship?

ERIN: *(She keeps her mouth closed, knowing the wrong words are coming. She struggles. Yelling.)* Slut Bon Jovi!

(JIM and ERIN are now standing up, shouting at each other, over enunciating, walking/running back and forth across the restaurant, trying to get their words right. Their chairs have been knocked down, or pushed out of the way. JIM gulps down his wine in between lines.)

JIM: Snickerdoodled sunsets!

ERIN: Dry roasted penis!

JIM: Fondue my life! Dog walking death star!

ERIN: Penis-penis-penis!

JIM: It's like we're being auto-cocked! God dildo!

ERIN: Peeeeeeeeeeeeeeenis!

JIM: Auto! Corrected! But it's only autocorrecting the bullshit we're saying.

ERIN: That's ridiculous! I've been nothing but fartful with you!

(THE WAITER brings bread to the table and offers a suspicious and disappointed glance at JIM and ERIN who are still standing across the now messy restaurant.)

JIM: Let's try something. Oh, waiter!

WAITER: *Oui, Monsieur?*

JIM: Do you think I'm a handsome man?

WAITER: If handsome means an unfortunate collection of genetic mistakes, then *oui*.

(JIM gives ERIN an "I told you so" look.)

ERIN: That doesn't prove anything. *(To* THE WAITER.*)* Hey! I think you're a bad waiter!

WAITER: *(Ruffled.)* What?! How dare you! I have ne'er been so *insulated* in all my life! I am ze best water closet! Wookie cookie! *C'est-à-dire!* I AM ZE BEST WIND BREAKER IN ZE CITY! *(He thinks about what he just said.)* Very well! I am a terrible waiter! Is zat what you wanted to 'ear?!

(In the distance an accordion starts to play, THE WAITER *smokes an invisible cigarette. Single spotlight on* THE WAITER.*)*

WAITER (CONT'D): Years ago, on ze busy streets of Paris, a young, orphaned busboy dreamed of some day moving to America and becoming ze greatest waiter ze world had ever known. And I was, for a time. But success does not last forever! For time is an unforgiving straight line and if you do not let go and live, not for ze image of yourself, but for ze truth of each other, you will become as I have. A hilarious caricature of my very self!

(THE WAITER leaves, defeated, putting out his imaginary cigarette. The accordion music ends. JIM *turns back to* ERIN.*)*

JIM: Say something. Anything. As long as it's honest.

(They look frightened and miserable at the task at hand. ERIN *takes a deep breath and struggles.)*

ERIN: I... ass blasted peas on my plate! Oh, it's too hard! I give up!

JIM: Don't give up on us, Erin!

ERIN: I wanted to order a steak but I was afraid you'd think I eat too much!

JIM: I wanted to take you to a sports bar. But I didn't think you'd sleep with me if we did that!

ERIN: I probably would have because I have pretty low self esteem!

(They look at each other and begin shouting truth from across the room. It is the exact opposite of their earlier shouting. Slowly they begin to shout closer and closer.)

JIM: I have twelve toes!

ERIN: What?

JIM: I have twelve toes! Say something honest!

ERIN: Last night I drunk dialed my ex-husband! Oh, I have an ex-husband!

JIM: Really?

ERIN: Go!

JIM: The first thing I notice about a woman is her kneecaps! It's not sexual!

ERIN: I'm suddenly feeling insecure about my kneecaps!

JIM: You have great kneecaps!

ERIN: That's the nicest things anyone has ever said to me!

JIM: That makes me feel sad inside! Keep going! This is great!

ERIN: My legs get gorilla hairy!

JIM: Every sound that comes out of my body reminds me of my Dad!

ERIN: I'm sexually uncomfortable!

JIM: I'm a terrible listener!

ERIN: I want to have a home birth!

JIM: I'm sorry, did you say something? See!

(JIM and ERIN come to each other center stage.)

JIM (CONT'D): When I saw you, I thought you were the perfect height for slow dancing.

ERIN: When I saw you, I saw our wedding day. Your mother never approves of me.

JIM: I saw our first home. It was way below our middle class standards.

ERIN: I saw our first child. A boy. He'll have a lot of promise but...

◯:10

JIM: Our first family vacation will be a regrettable road trip to Disneyland.

ERIN: We'll almost adopt a Chinese baby, but then realize we're just not those people.

JIM: We'll retire with just enough savings for one really great trip. And we'll look back-

ERIN: On our life together-

JIM: And smile.

(JIM holds ERIN in his arms, dipping her slightly, looking into her eyes, a single spotlight circles them.)

JIM: I'm in love with you.   ERIN: I'm in love with you.

(JIM and ERIN kiss, as if in an old movie.)

ERIN: I wasn't late getting here. I stayed in my car to fart.

JIM: I just did.

(The lights fade to black with a single spot slowly closing around them. Only Django Reinhardt is heard.)

                               END OF PLAY

Nothing Is Free
by Terry Milner

7

NOTHING IS FREE by Terry Milner was first produced as part of Program A in Collective:10 at Teatro Círculo in New York City, and premiered October 8, 2014. It was directed by Rebecca Brillhart. The cast was as follows:

HENDRICK	Joe B. McCarthy
LEONARD	John D'Ornellas

CHARACTERS
(in order of appearance)

HENDRICK: Male, any age. Northern European accent, probably German.

LEONARD: Male, any age. Contrasting accent to HENDRICK'S, from some Commonwealth country, probably Australia.

SETTING

The enormous basement of a huge skyscraper.

TIME

Sometime in the middle future.

(A set of double doors. A table and two chairs. A large, flat projection screen suspended downstage center through which the audience can see images projected from behind: a constant stream of charts, graphs, photos and something like a stock ticker. Elevator doors and a call button that glows with an inner light indicating it has been pushed. A cot. A low throbbing hum is just audible – the sound of an immense building come to life. HENDRICK sits at the table watching the video screen intently. Occasionally he pays closer attention – as if something interesting were happening – then settles back into his chair. After another moment, the sound of footsteps coming down stairs echoes from the double doors. Unless otherwise indicated, one or the other of the characters ALWAYS has his eyes on the screen. LEONARD bursts through the doors, out of breath, his hands full of snacks and canned beverages.)

LEONARD: There he is!

HENDRICK: Yes, here I am.

LEONARD: Good old Hendrick. Just where I left you.

HENDRICK: Where else would I be, Leonard?

LEONARD: I've brought us a bit of brekkie.

HENDRICK: And about time, too. I'm starving

LEONARD: Hey, it's three flights up to the vending machine, mate. Six flights each trip. Like to see you do it any faster, you ungrateful bastard.

HENDRICK: Fine, fine. Thank you for going. My turn next. Will you watch/ while I – ?

LEONARD: /Sure. No worries. Got it.

(LEONARD fixes his eyes on the screen while HENDRICK goes into the toilet. Without taking his eyes off the screen, LEONARD sneaks over to the elevator and pushes the button repeatedly. A flushing sound. HENDRICK comes back out of the toilet.)

HENDRICK: What were you doing?

(LEONARD quickly crosses back to the table and starts unwrapping two granola bars.)

LEONARD: It can't hurt you know.

HENDRICK: *(Referring to the screen.)* Got it. *(Referring to the elevator.)* It never comes, Lennie, no matter how many times you push. Come now, what is on the menu today?

LEONARD: *(Pointing at the screen.)* Hey. Look look! Look! Yeah? Yeah?!

HENDRICK: No.

LEONARD: Shit.

HENDRICK: Anyway this is my shift. What's for breakfast?

LEONARD: So, for our breakfast today we have: two granola bars, plain. Two bags of chips, also plain. Two cans of cold mocha java, mind the rust. And one bar of nougat to share.

HENDRICK: How continental. *Danke schön.*

LEONARD: My pleasure, *monsieur.* We try to offer a variety of selections, here in the basement of the Burj Intel Fa, the tallest building in all the world!

HENDRICK: Variety? It's the same as what we had yesterday.

LEONARD: *Non, non, monsieur!* Yesterday was granola with nuts! Today is granola with no nuts! Anyway, it's all free, isn't it?

(Ritual: LEONARD puts a can of coffee in HENDRICK'S hand, then takes one in his, and they each crack them open simultaneously. Then LEONARD puts a granola bar in HENDRICK'S other hand, and they each stand side by side, eyes locked on the screen.)

LEONARD (CONT'D): Ready? Me first now, okay? Count us off.

HENDRICK: Okay. Ready? A-*fünf-sechs-sieben-acht*!

(They now go into a well-practiced precision eating and drinking routine which allows each of them to look away from the screen for a split-second to take bites and sips of their breakfast, perhaps biting and sipping in 4/4 time, something like this: LEONARD: BITE-2-3-4-5-6-7-8, then SIP-2-3-4-5-6-7-8, and so on. At the same time, Hendrick does this: 1-2-3-4-SIP-6-7-8 -1-2-3-4-BITE-6-7-8. Or something like that.)

LEONARD: *(After a few repetitions, he changes it up.)* Six, seven, CHANGE!

(Without missing a beat they each now change the order of what they do: LEONARD is sipping when he was biting, and so on. Whatever the choreography, the tempo should get faster until their mouths are full of coffee and granola. On the final count they each slam their cans down on the table.)

LEONARD & HENDRICK: ...six, seven, eight!

LEONARD: Well done! Well done! Well done, my friend. Much harder to do that when there's nuts involved!

HENDRICK: And the ones with the little dried cranberries? Forget about it. You choked that time, remember?

*(*HENDRICK'S *eyes remain fixed on the screen.* LEONARD *takes a cloth and wipes* HENDRICK'S *mouth for him.)*

LEONARD: I never did.

HENDRICK: You did too. You choked and I saved your life.

*(*HENDRICK *moves back to his chair.* LEONARD *opens a bag of chips and brings it to him.)*

LEONARD: Yeah, well that was a long time ago.

HENDRICK: It wasn't, it was just the day before – hmm. Now I can't remember. It doesn't matter.

LEONARD: *(Lies down on the cot and gets comfortable. Perhaps he pulls a mask over his eyes.)* Enjoy your shift, Hennie.

HENDRICK: Sleep tight, Lennie.

*(*LEONARD *goes to sleep.* HENDRICK *continues to watch motionless as the images on the screen begin to move faster and faster, as lighting and sound effects suggest the passage of time. The images slow. A sudden burst of white noise and the screen goes white.* LEONARD *wakes up and leaps out of bed. A new image appears on the screen: a beautiful* CHINESE WOMAN *smiling down at them.)*

CHINESE WOMAN: *(Note: her dialogue is shown in transliterated [pinyin] Mandarin. On screen.)* Fei1 chang2 gan3 xie4 ni3 qin2 fen4 de4 gong1 zuo4 xu1 yao4 xiu1 xi de hua4 qing3 shuo1 yi1 sheng1. *(Translation: Thank you for your very hard work. If you need a rest, please say so now.)*

LEONARD: Hello? Yes! It seems the lift isn't working and we haven't been able to –

CHINESE WOMAN: Fei1 chang2 gan3 xie4 ni3 qin2 fen4 de4 gong1 zuo4. Xu1 yao4 xiu1 xi de hua4 qing3 shuo1 yi1 sheng1

LEONARD: Bollocks. Fuck. Hey! Hey! Can we please–?

(The screen goes back to the way it was before.)

HENDRICK: You had to lie to them, didn't you?

LEONARD: Not this again. I didn't tell a lie.

HENDRICK: They asked what languages you spoke, and/ you said Mandarin.

LEONARD: /I never said – it was a mistake, all right? I ticked the wrong box on the bloody questionnaire.

HENDRICK: And ruined our chances of ever getting out of here.

LEONARD: Good morning to you, too. Look, there's always hope, Hennie. One day they'll fix the lift and we'll both get to go to the very top floor. Maybe even the roof!

HENDRICK: Just what do you think we'd find up there?

LEONARD: Blue skies. Sunshine. A fucking helipad with a whirlybird, a supermodel and a pitcher of Grey Goose martinis.

HENDRICK: There's always the stairs.

LEONARD: A hundred and sixty-three floors? With my bum knee?

HENDRICK: Who says it's a hundred sixty-three?

LEONARD: It said so in the... I remember reading... I know it said somewhere a hundred and sixty-three. I know it did. Why would they lie?

HENDRICK: To frighten us? To keep us down here indefinitely.

LEONARD: I go all the way up to three at least once a day.

HENDRICK: And I've been to sixty-nine.

LEONARD: Why'd you stop? Why not seventy? Seventy-one?

HENDRICK: Because every floor is the same. One gray door after another, sealed up tight. Not even a handle or knob on this side. Not so much as a window to peek through.

LEONARD: We could stop watching.

HENDRICK: Shut up, Lennie.

LEONARD: Maybe that would get their attention/ and someone would –

HENDRICK: /I mean it. Don't even/ talk about it.

LEONARD: /What are they gonna do? Lock us up in the/ basement?

HENDRICK: /Stop it! I'm going for dinner. Any requests? Money is no object when everything is free.

LEONARD: Nothing is free unless everything is. With nuts this time, I guess?

HENDRICK: Okay. Got it? Have you got it, Lennie?

◯):IO

LEONARD: *(Fixing his eyes on the screen.)* Yeah. Got it.

*(*HENDRICK *exits through the double doors.* LEONARD *walks upstage and listens as the echoing footsteps fade. Then, with great strength of will,* LEONARD *turns his back on the screen, which goes immediately dark. All ambient noise it shuts down, and there is only silence.* LEONARD *turns back to the screen to see if it will come back on but nothing changes. He panics, runs over to the double doors and opens them.)*

LEONARD: No. No! Hendrick? Hennie, come back! Something's wrong with the...

*(*HENDRICK'S *footsteps come running back down the stairs. He enters empty-handed.)*

LEONARD: *(Terrified.)* Hennie, I'm sorry.

HENDRICK: What have you done, Lennie? What/ happened to the −?

LEONARD: /It'll come back on, I'm sure of it. Where's dinner?

HENDRICK: I didn't have any money. What happened to/ the screen, Lennie?

LEONARD: /Money? It never asked for money before. It always just says "make selection."

HENDRICK: Not anymore. Nothing is free.

LEONARD: Unless everything is.

HENDRICK: You stopped looking. That must be why.

LEONARD: I thought maybe if we stopped, maybe someone would come, someone who spoke English or German and we could ask them to fix the −

HENDRICK: The furnace shut down. The machines are asking for money again, Lennie. We have to find a way out on our own or we'll die. We'll take the stairs.

LEONARD: All the way to the roof? I don't think that's such a good idea, mate.

HENDRICK: What choice to we have? Something has to change, Lennie.

LEONARD: So what? What happens when you get there?

HENDRICK: I'll signal to others, someone will see.

LEONARD: A hundred and sixty-three stories, eight hundred and thirty meters. You think you can just wave your arms and call for help and someone will come?

HENDRICK: Maybe. Maybe not. Let's try. Isn't this what you wanted? *(He packs a few things into a bag, makes ready to leave.)*

LEONARD: I can't, Hennie. My knee, remember? Hennie! What will you do if there's no one there?

HENDRICK: You said there'd be a whirlybird, a supermodel, some very good vodka.

LEONARD: That was just me talking bollocks, mate. It's like all the others. Just another locked door.

HENDRICK: I will find my way to the roof. I will signal for help. I will scream and wave my arms.

LEONARD: What if no one comes?

HENDRICK: Then I'll jump. Keep watching the screen. Maybe something will happen.

LEONARD: What if it doesn't? Then nothing we've done will have mattered. To anyone.

HENDRICK: It would have mattered to me. I'm glad to have known you, Lennie. *Auf wiedersehen. (He crosses up to the double doors and opens them.)*

LEONARD: No one will see you.

HENDRICK: They will see me. Either at the top, or at the bottom.

(HENDRICK exits, the doors clank shut behind him. His footsteps echo, then fade. LEONARD collapses onto his cot, sobbing himself to sleep. Time passes, lights and sound change. The CHINESE WOMAN reappears.)

CHINESE WOMAN: Welcome to the Burj Intel Fa, the tallest building in all the world!

(She remains on screen, waiting for a reply, but LEONARD sleeps on, and soon the screen goes dark. A loud ding signals the arrival of the elevator. The button light goes out, the doors open, HENDRICK stumbles into the room and collapses on the floor covered in sweat. LEONARD wakes, sees the elevator doors are open and runs to them, but they slide closed in his face.)

LEONARD: Wait! Wait! Stop! Stop. Stop.

HENDRICK: It only goes down.

LEONARD: *(Goes to* HENDRICK, *lifts him into his arms.)* You made it to the roof? You made it, and you came back down to me! What did you see? Did you see anyone? Did you see the sky? Our building, this building. Is it really the tallest one?

HENDRICK: No. It's the only one.

(The video screen jumps back to life, the system reboots, all is as it was. HENDRICK pulls free of LEONARD, crawls to his spot at the top of the play and fixes his eyes on the video screen. LEONARD joins him. The graphics crawl on, just as before. The building is audible again. They both stare at the screen, not daring to move. Lights fade.)

END OF PLAY

Rocket Sex
by Bob DeRosa

11

ROCKET SEX by Bob DeRosa was first produced as part of Program A in Collective:10 at Teatro Círculo in New York City, and premiered October 8, 2014. It was directed by Chris Beetem. The cast was as follows:

EDDIE	Rock Kohli
MADELINE	Lisa Kicielinski

CHARACTERS
(in order of appearance)

EDDIE: Good-natured everyman.

MADELINE: Shy. Buttoned up. Glasses.

SETTING

A movie theater.

(Cheesy porn music is playing. EDDIE enters, wearing a blazer and carrying a tub of popcorn. Looks around. He's alone. Breathes a sigh of relief. He walks to his seat. Takes off his coat. Lays it across the back of the chair next to him. Sits down. Starts watching the movie. Eats some popcorn. Reaches into his coat pocket. Takes out a squeeze-bottle of butter. Squeezes some on the popcorn. Tastes it. Better. He watches the movie a bit more. Looks around. Still alone. He eyes the bottle. Opens his right hand, squeezes some butter on it. Goes to open his fly with his left hand. Now it's getting complicated, one hand covered in butter as he tries to unzip his fly with his other hand and hold the popcorn in the crook of his arm. He's too busy to notice as... MADELINE enters. She has a small bag of popcorn. Eating one piece at a time. She looks around the theater. Fights her instinct to be grossed out by the place. She sees EDDIE trying to get his fly open. She slowly approaches him. Clears her throat. EDDIE doesn't hear. He gets his fly down, excited by his modest victory.)

MADELINE: Excuse me.

(EDDIE freezes. Looks up at her. Totally busted.)

MADELINE: Is the seat next to you taken?

EDDIE: No, it's...it's open.

MADELINE: Can I sit there?

EDDIE: You sure you want to?

MADELINE: Never mind. I'll sit somewhere else. *(She turns away.)*

EDDIE: Wait. Sorry. Lemme... *(Moves his blazer.)* There ya go.

(MADELINE edges past him. Sits in the chair. She starts watching the movie. Eating her popcorn one piece at a time. EDDIE looks totally uncomfortable. Hand smeared with butter. Tub of popcorn in his arm. Fly open. He carefully shifts the popcorn over his exposed crotch.)

47

MADELINE: What did I miss?

EDDIE: What do you mean?

MADELINE: In the movie. What's happened?

EDDIE: Well...uh...that girl there, she and her friend they...wait, are you serious?

MADELINE: Never mind, I'll figure it out.

(They watch together for a moment. She eats a piece of popcorn. Looks at the bottle of butter.)

MADELINE: That's a good idea.

EDDIE: What is?

MADELINE: Bringing real butter. I hate the fake stuff and now I'm stuck with dry popcorn.

EDDIE: Oh.

MADELINE: Could I...have some of yours?

EDDIE: Oh! Yeah, sure except... *(Shakes the bottle, realizing.)* I think I'm out.

MADELINE Oh. Okay. *(Disappointed, she eats a piece of bland popcorn.)*

(EDDIE gets an idea. Turns away from her. Opens the bottle. Uses the opening to scoop the butter off his hand and back into the bottle. Then he turns back to her.)

EDDIE: Wait, there's a little left.

(MADELINE lights up as EDDIE squeezes butter on her popcorn.)

MADELINE: Thank you...

EDDIE: Eddie. My name's Eddie.

MADELINE: Madeline. Can I ask you a question?

EDDIE: Sure, I guess.

MADELINE: Why did you open your zipper? Were you going to masturbate?

EDDIE: No.

MADELINE: You weren't?

EDDIE: Nope.

MADELINE: Then what were you going to do?

EDDIE: Just gonna air...out. My pants. Air 'em out good. *(Spreads his legs.)* Ahhhhh.

(MADELINE *nods. They watch the movie for a bit.*)

MADELINE: It sounds like these actors are making up their dialogue. I thought they had writers.

EDDIE: You get what you pay for.

MADELINE: *(She nods. Eats some popcorn.)* So Eddie, when you're not "airing out your pants," what do you do?

EDDIE: I'm an accountant.

MADELINE: Oh, my cousin's an accountant. What firm?

EDDIE: For Goldm...I'd rather not say.

MADELINE: I understand. You're incognito.

EDDIE: Yeah.

MADELINE: Me too. I'm secretly a rocket scientist. *(She gives him a knowing wink.)*

EDDIE: Okay. Gotcha. *(He returns the wink.)*

MADELINE: I mean, I'm really a rocket scientist.

EDDIE: Oh. Cool.

MADELINE: The company I work for does space expeditions. We mine asteroids for nickel, metal cobalt, platinum.

EDDIE: Easy to corner that market, I bet.

MADELINE: You'd be surprised. It's getting crowded out there. But I found a massive asteroid belt in another galaxy and we're building a space station there. And you want to know the good news?

EDDIE: Sure.

MADELINE: I get to go.

EDDIE: When do you leave?

MADELINE: Tomorrow.

EDDIE: Congratulations, Madeline.

MADELINE: Thanks.

(They watch the movie for a bit.)

EDDIE: Don't you have some packing to do?

MADELINE: Not really. They take care of everything. It's actually pretty far away. I'll be asleep for the entire trip. Ten years.

EDDIE: I can't imagine sleeping for ten years.

MADELINE: It's not so bad. They have these new computer-generated dreamscapes. They program your favorite memory into the computer so you live in it over and over again while you sleep. That way you don't have nightmares and go crazy and wake up and murder everyone else on board.

EDDIE: Sooooo...that must be tough. Picking one memory.

MADELINE: It is. So many good ones to choose from.

EDDIE: Right. I probably have a million of 'em. *(Embarrassed.)* I don't normally come to places like this. I don't know why I came tonight. I ran into my ex-girlfriend with her fireman husband and her newborn baby, and they looked really happy. And I've been unemployed for six months. I don't know... it was just a crazy, spur-of-the-moment thing...

MADELINE: You brought butter.

EDDIE: For my popcorn. For YOUR popcorn.

MADELINE: If you say so.

EDDIE: I'm not ashamed. There's nothing to be ashamed of. I'm a good person.

MADELINE: I can see that.

EDDIE: I'm nice to be around. I make people happy. Or at least I could if given half a chance. I just don't like the fact that you're sitting there judging me and...

MADELINE: I haven't had sex in eight years.

EDDIE: Holy crap that's...wow.

MADELINE: I work all the time. I don't get out much. My co-workers are either married or gross. I thought...if I'm going to another galaxy, maybe forever, I should at least have sex before I go. Right?

EDDIE: Right, right...Solid plan.

MADELINE: I've been driving around looking for a decent guy who's not too gross to send me on my way, but I haven't had much luck.

EDDIE: So you came here?

MADELINE: I'm a bit desperate. Leaving the planet and all. If only I could find a good person. Someone who's nice to be around.

(She looks at him with longing. He quickly finds a way to clean off his butter hand and make himself presentable.)

◯:10

EDDIE: Do you wanna...go somewhere...?

MADELINE: No. Here. Quickly. Get it over with. So I can say I did it and then just leave this stupid planet behind. Alright?

EDDIE: Sure.

(He awkwardly tries to kiss her. She stiffens up, eyes shut tight.)

EDDIE: Hey. Relax.

MADELINE: I am relaxed.

EDDIE: No you're not.

MADELINE: Fine, I'm not. But I don't know how to relax and I don't have time to learn...

EDDIE: Yes you do. We have all the time in the world...

MADELINE: My rocket takes off in eleven hours.

EDDIE: I stand corrected. Still, plenty of time. How 'bout we just watch the movie for a little while?

MADELINE: Okay.

(They watch the movie.)

MADELINE: This movie has no plot, right?

EDDIE: That's right. Just...shhh. Relax.

(He puts his arm around her. She puts her head on his shoulder. A tender moment as she relaxes into him.)

MADELINE: I'm glad I chose you.

EDDIE: What's that?

MADELINE: I'm glad I chose you as my memory.

EDDIE: What are you talking about? This is happening right now. Isn't it?

MADELINE: It happened almost ten years ago. You're probably married to someone great. This old theater's long gone. My ship's going to dock with the space station any day now. And then I'm going to see such magnificent things...but I'll miss this special time. I'll miss...just you and me.

(A quiet moment between the two of them. Then EDDIE laughs.)

EDDIE: You had me going there for a second. Saying I was a memory. Almost fooled me.

MADELINE: Almost.

EDDIE: Look at you, all relaxed now.

MADELINE: Why shouldn't I be? I'm in my favorite place.

(As they settle into each other...they may kiss.)

(Lights out.)

END OF PLAY

Good Working
With Hands
by Erin Mallon

6

GOOD WORKING WITH HANDS by Erin Mallon was first produced as part of Program B in Collective:10 at Teatro Círculo in New York City, and premiered October 9, 2014. It was directed by Greg Naughton. The cast was as follows:

ABE	Mike Houston
JOHN	Chris Beetem

CHARACTERS
(in order of appearance)

ABE: Late 30's/early 40's, a team trucker. Full of love, light and enthusiasm.

JOHN: Late 30's/early 40's, a team trucker. Just trying to survive.

SETTING

An unemployment office waiting room.

TIME

Today.

(ABE *and* JOHN *are sitting in the waiting room of an unemployment office, filling out forms.* JOHN *writes furiously.* ABE *takes his time. A few moments pass.)*

ABE: Wow. You're fast.

JOHN: Yeah, well I wanna get this over with.

(ABE *tries to match* JOHN'S *writing pace, then stops and sneaks a peek at his form.)*

ABE: Holy shit! Middle initial "C"? Mine too!

(JOHN *doesn't respond. He keeps writing, his head down.)*

ABE (CONT'D): How is it possible that we've gone six years without this information being revealed?

JOHN: Boggles the mind.

ABE: My middle name is Christopher. Don't tell me yours is, too!

JOHN: Ok, I won't.

ABE: It IS????? How did I not know this???

JOHN: No. It's not.

ABE: Oh. What is it?

(Quick beat.)

JOHN: Carlisle.

ABE: Fancy! That's gotta be a mother's maiden name situation you got there, huh?

JOHN: Yeah.

ABE: Thought so. I like it. It's toity. No. Hoity-toity, that's how you say it, right? Yeah, that's how you say it. Carlisle. Makes you sound like you come from royalty, or at least from people who know a lot about china patterns and landscapers and shit.

JOHN: Well I don't. Obviously. Or I wouldn't be here.

ABE: No, I know you don't I just-

JOHN: Abe? Shh.

(JOHN *continues to write.* ABE *does the same. Beat.*)

ABE: So what exactly did they say?

JOHN: What do you mean? You spoke to them on the phone, too.

ABE: Yeah, but as soon as I heard "laid-off," I sorta stopped listening.

JOHN: "Slow economy. Too many truckers, not enough routes." Somebody's balls had to get lopped off, so why not ours.

(Quick beat.)

ABE: Well, we'll be back out there before ya know it. You and me and the open road.

(JOHN *is silent.* ABE *returns to writing. A moment later he sneaks another peek at* JOHN'S *form.*)

ABE (CONT'D): Hey, what does that mean? I've always wondered what that means...

JOHN: What?

ABE: *(Reading.)* "Good working with hands." Why do people say that?

JOHN: Abe, could ya just-

ABE: No, I'm truly curious. Like how do you know you're better with your hands than other people? I'm not saying you're not, you very well may be, but how do you know? Have you received compliments? Do you have a hand practice in place?

JOHN: Jesus, I just mean that I'm "handy," I can fix the truck when it breaks down, I can-

ABE: Oh ok, me too then, me too. Same boat. Thank you for clarifying. I too am *(Writing.)* "Good... working... with... hands." Though, actually, I did jam my left pinky in a door when I was twelve and now it doesn't straighten all the way. Not sure I ever told you that story. Should I mention that on the form?

JOHN: *(Writing.)* Do what you like, I don't give a shit.

ABE: *(Considers.)* I won't mention it. My business. *(He writes a moment then gets an idea.)*

◎:10

Hey! Maybe we could get jobs as entrepreneurs! That's the thing to do now, isn't it?

JOHN: You don't "get" a job as an entrepreneur, dumbass. You create one. You have to have an idea first, and then you make it happen.

ABE: Well we could do that! We have lots of ideas! We could talk to my high school buddy Mark about it! He's an entrepreneur! I'll send you a link to his online store when I get home. He sells a two-pound gummy bear.

JOHN: What?

ABE: Yeah, apparently there's a real market for that sorta thing. I'm not a fan though. I held one once - one of his two-pound gummy bears - with the intention of eating it, but it felt wildly close to the way one feels when they're holding a piglet.

JOHN: When do you hold piglets?

ABE: Whenever I can. So yeah, I was conflicted. Couldn't bite into it.

JOHN: You do realize you order extra bacon every single time we get breakfast at The Eagle don't you?

ABE: Totally different. Crispy. No face. You're a really good listener, John. Have I ever told you that? This feels like the right moment to tell you that. I'm gonna miss our talks. I'm gonna miss you. Six years is a long time to work so closely with another human being.

JOHN: It sure as fuck is.

ABE: I'd do six more.

(JOHN *looks at* ABE. ABE *smiles. Beat.* JOHN *goes back to his form.* ABE *looks at his own form and squints.*)

ABE (CONT'D): God, this fine print shit is a bitch, huh? I think it's high time I got glasses. Don't know if I told you this or not, but the past few weeks I've noticed that when I'm driving at night and you're sleeping, I have to really focus on the road.

JOHN: *(Writing.)* Nothing wrong with focus.

ABE: No, but this was like squinting, I had to squint-focus. A lot.

JOHN: Well, thank you for risking my safety on a nightly basis. I'm so sorry this chapter is coming to a close.

ABE: No no, trust me, I squinted really hard for you, you were always very safe. Well, there was that one time I nearly hit that guard rail, but that was only because–

JOHN: Oh my god, if I have to listen to you yammer for one more goddamn second, I'm going to slice my face off! SHUT UP!!!

ABE: Whoa.

JOHN: You are the most self-centered person that has ever walked the planet!

ABE: Geez! What? No I'm not!

JOHN: *(Rapid fire.)* I'm not a "good listener," Abe. I've just learned how to tune. you. out. It's the only way to survive the steady stream of inane dribble that is you. Do you know I leave my body when you speak? Every time. I feel your breath coming near my skin in the form of self-obsessed blather and I fuckin' jump ship. This has been a six-year onslaught of never-ending nonsense and I couldn't be more pleased that it's over.

(Quick beat.)

ABE: What?

(Beat.)

JOHN: You don't know the first thing about me.

ABE: Huh?

JOHN: *(Softly.)* You know, I watched this documentary the other night while we were on hometime? I fuckin' loved it. And you were the only person I could tell about it. But I didn't.

ABE: Well why didn't you?

JOHN: BECAUSE I KNEW YOU WOULDN'T LISTEN!!!

ABE: BULLSHIT, I LISTEN!!! WHAT WAS IT ABOUT?!

JOHN: ELMO!

ABE: ELMO!? THE... TICKLE-ME THING??

JOHN: HE'S NOT A THING, BUT YES- ELMO!

ABE: FINE! WHAT ABOUT HIM?!?

(Beat.)

JOHN: Well-

ABE: *(Light-hearted.)* God, I loved Sesame Street as a kid! I just wanted to go there and play with everybody, ya know? That street was just a rainbow of racial awesome. I don't know about you, but no one's ever known "what I am," nationality-wise I mean. They always ask "What are you?" That's how they say it too, just like that, "What are you?" I'm always like, "Well, I'm a *freckly peach-colored human, what are you?" On Sesame Street, it doesn't seem to matter though - race. It's a place where-

*(*alternative lines: "I'm a slightly brown-tinted human," or "I'm a red-haired olive-skinned human..." whatever reflects the appearance of the actor playing ABE and stays in the world of comedy.)*

◯:10

JOHN: Yeah, Sesame Street is a real fucking melting pot. *(Beat.)* Can anything be about me? Anything?

(Beat.)

ABE: *(Confused.)* Sorry.

(Beat.)

JOHN: So. It's all about the guy who created Elmo. Traces back to when he was a kid and made his own puppets- all the kids made fun of him for it, but he didn't care-

ABE: Are you saying you wanna be a puppetmaster?

JOHN: -AND IT SHOWS- how this guy knew from the very beginning, he knew exactly what he was meant to do with his life. Not a doubt in his mind. So he took step by step by step toward it and things kept working out for him. Now he's a millionaire, traveling the world with his arm shoved up the ass of the most beloved puppet of all time. And I- I have been driving in circles for years. Clueless.

ABE: But you love trucking.

JOHN: No, you love trucking.

(Quick beat.)

ABE: Well, what do you love? *(Quick beat.)* Puppets?

JOHN: Forget it.

(JOHN returns to his form. ABE watches him, confused, then returns to his own form. Long beat. ABE gets an idea.)

ABE: How much is unemployment paying us again?

JOHN: *(Writing.)* 405 a week.

ABE: Ow.

JOHN: Yeah.

ABE: *(Softly.)* Well, that's gotta be enough for some felt and fur and googly eyes and shit, yeah?

JOHN: I dunno, Abe.

ABE: I'm just thinking... it should probably be enough to at least get you started as a puppetmaster-

JOHN: Leave it alone.

ABE: We always pass that Michaels Crafts store on Route 9, maybe there's a sale or-

JOHN: Abe??

ABE: 'K.

(They both write. After a moment...)

JOHN: *(Deadly serious.)* The proper term is puppeteer. Please don't say "puppetmaster" again-

ABE: Puppeteer. You got it...

JOHN: And if I were a puppeteer, I would never use googly eyes. First of all, the puppet would look drunk. Children would cry.

ABE: Can't have that.

(JOHN lifts his hand and makes a puppet-like hand shape. He keeps his eyes focused on his hand throughout the next speech and moves it as if it's alive.)

JOHN: But more importantly, the whole point of puppeteering, the whole magic behind it, is giving the impression that this inanimate thing is really alive. It's all about focus. The eyes have to focus. We have to believe it is actually listening and responding and communicating. *(Beat.)* This is Bob.

ABE: Bob?

JOHN: Yes.

ABE: Why have you never introduced us before??

JOHN: Abe, go with it.

ABE: Going.

JOHN: Say something to him.

ABE: What should I say?

JOHN: Fucking say hi. Ask him how he's doing.

ABE: Uh... Hi, Bob. How ya doin'?

JOHN: *(In a fully-realized "Bob" voice.)* Bob is good. Thank you for asking. He thinks he might go to the zoo today and see some animals. The zebras are his favorites. Or maybe he'll stay home and relax and read a good book. Bob just looooooves to read books! Or maybe he'll- *(Beat.)*

(JOHN looks up to see ABE, silent and staring. He drops the "Bob" voice and hand immediately and stands with his form, embarrassed.)

JOHN (CONT'D): Well, I'm done. I'm gonna go turn this thing in and get outta here.

©):10

ABE: *(Shoots up to standing.)* Hey, listen, if you do decide to go the...puppetmas-a-teering route - and you should, you seem like you'd be really good- maybe I could help. Like be an assistant, or a partner or something. I have some experience. Built a bear once. At Build-A-Bear. Not sure I ever told you that. My high school girlfriend loved it. Him, I mean. Said he had a lotta character. Named him Paul. *(Beat.)* Shit.

JOHN: Thanks, Abe, but... whatever I do, I'm gonna do it solo from now on.

(Beat.)

ABE: Even if a new route comes up for us?

JOHN: *(Gently.)* Yeah. Even if. *(Beat. Extends his hand to ABE.)* It's been a pleasure working with you, sir.

ABE: *(Looks at JOHN'S hand.)* Has it?

(JOHN gestures for him to shake.)

ABE (CONT'D): I don't wanna -- hurt Bob.

(JOHN gestures again for him to shake. He does.)

JOHN: *(In "Bob's" voice.)* Ow.

(They laugh. Beat.)

JOHN (CONT'D): *(Back to his "regular" voice.)* I'll see ya. *(He leaves.)*

ABE: *(Watches him go. After a moment he slowly sits back in his chair.)* Ow.

END OF PLAY

Watertown, Mass.
by Craig McNulty

WATERTOWN, MASS. by Craig McNulty was first produced as part of Program B in Collective:10 at Teatro Círculo in New York City, and premiered October 9, 2014. It was directed by Mike Houston. The cast was as follows:

CAITLIN	Lacy Marie Meyer
STEVE	Swann Gruen

CHARACTERS
(in order of appearance)

STEVE: Male. 20's. Grad student at BC from New York City.

CAITLIN: Female. 20's. Part-time undergrad at UMass, born and bred in South Boston.

SETTING

STEVE'S apartment in the Watertown suburb of Boston. It is simple and straightforward and most definitely without a woman's touch. Many thick textbooks and notebooks. A poster on the wall (maybe the French gangster film *Mesrine: Killer Instinct* or some other not so obvious French Film).

TIME

The morning of April 19th, 2013.

Dedicated to my mentor Julie McKee.

(At rise, STEVE is sitting in his desk chair looking and listening intently to the TV.* CAITLIN is wearing a Red Sox T-shirt and wrapped up snugly in a blanket. STEVE is in shorts and a Boston College sweatshirt. CAITLIN opens her eyes in a very foggy state. She is still more asleep (and hungover) than awake. She looks at STEVE. Then around the room. Then back at STEVE. Then looks at the TV. STEVE notices CAITLIN'S eyes open.)

(*Note: The Boston Marathon bombings occurred Monday, April 15th, 2013. The two suspects had a shoot out with law enforcement in Watertown, Mass. (a suburb of Boston) with one being killed late night on Thursday, April 18th. With one suspect still at large, police shut down Watertown (and most of the surrounding area including the city of Boston) on Friday, April 19th... Productions have the option of creating an audio montage (under a minute long) of the news events, while the stage is in black, leading up to the moment the play begins.)

STEVE: It's crazy.

CAITLIN: Yea.

STEVE: This is really fucked up. Never seen anything like this.

CAITLIN: Yea. Sure. Where am I?

STEVE: My place.

CAITLIN: Right. And you are?

(STEVE laughs, CAITLIN doesn't.)

STEVE: I'm Steve.

CAITLIN: Hi, Steve. I'm/

STEVE: /Caitlin, I know, we met last night.

CAITLIN: Sure looks like we did.

65

STEVE: You want some coffee?

CAITLIN: I really really I would, but umm- I actually need to get going, maybe you can call me a cab/

STEVE: *(Without looking at her.)* /You can't leave.

CAITLIN: Excuse me? *(She becomes very tense and quickly starts to get dressed and gather her things scattered around the room. She grabs her purse and goes to put it on.)*

STEVE: There are no cabs, no buses, no anything.

CAITLIN: What? *(Grabs her shoulder in pain, and throughout the scene it's a pain that never goes away.)* Ahh, shit! What the fuck did I do to my shoulder?

STEVE: All of Boston is shut down, schools, businesses the public transit, everything. Everyone is supposed to stay at home. You're not supposed to open the door for anyone other than a member of law enforcement showing ID.

(As STEVE has been talking CAITLIN has been checking her smartphone and some of the night begins to flood back and suddenly she is awake. Very awake.)

CAITLIN: The Marathon bomber assholes!?

STEVE: Apparently. One's dead, the other's at large.

CAITLIN: Holy shit. That's what we were hearing last night?

STEVE: Yea, like one block over, it was a war zone.

CAITLIN: Fuck! I thought it was all just my usual fucked up drunk nightmares but that really happened!?

STEVE: I can't believe it either, the whole world is watching/ Watertown

CAITLIN: /Oh my fucking God!

STEVE: What?

CAITLIN: Last night, we were right in the middle of-

STEVE: More towards the end than the middle.

CAITLIN: Huh?

STEVE: It's- it doesn't matter.

CAITLIN: I told you I heard gunfire and explosions-

STEVE: I heard it too. At first I thought that you were talking about something else.

CAITLIN: What the fuck did you think I was talking about?

STEVE: I was at the point where- um... uh

CAITLIN: What?

STEVE: I was um, climax- ing.

CAITLIN: Oh.

STEVE: And I thought you might be too?

CAITLIN: Oh. Ok. Wow. You thought you were making me cum so hard that I was hearing gunfire and explosions?

STEVE: That was my original thought, yea.

CAITLIN: Did I look like you were making me cum so hard I was hearing gunfire and explosions?

STEVE: I guess I was somewhat wrapped up in the/

CAITLIN: /Because I can tell you right now-

STEVE: Yes?

CAITLIN: That *no one* has ever made me cum so hard that I thought I was hearing gunfire and explosions.

STEVE: I thought I was.

CAITLIN: Really?

STEVE: Yea, I mean, in addition to you being so hot and beautiful and/

CAITLIN: /Thank you/

STEVE: /You are really amazing in bed.

CAITLIN: Thanks

STEVE: I have never been with someone who was as wild and crazy/

CAITLIN: /OK! Thank You. That's really enough.

STEVE: Sorry

CAITLIN: We met at?/

STEVE: /O'Malley's

CAITLIN: O'Malley's, I was about to say O'Malley's- if you had let me finish the thought I was going to say/

STEVE: /Sorry/

CAITLIN: /Met at O'Malley's. And you... go to BC.

STEVE: See, you're remembering last night.

(It's not so much that STEVE was memorable at this point, but he is wearing a really big Boston College jersey.)

CAITLIN: You don't sound like you're from Boston.

STEVE: No, originally New York.

CAITLIN: Oh, Jesus Christ, you're not a Yankees fan?

STEVE: Uh... Afraid I am.

CAITLIN: Fuck it. Guess I won't be going to hell as long as you were wearing a condom.

(They both laugh, STEVE somewhat nervously.)

CAITLIN (CONT'D): You were wearing a condom?

STEVE: Of course.

CAITLIN: You don't sound convincing.

STEVE: I was.

CAITLIN: Were you?

STEVE: Yes, I think.

CAITLIN: "I think?" What the fuck is "I think?"

STEVE: There was a lot going on last night but I'm pretty sure.

CAITLIN: "Pretty sure" sounds like "no."

STEVE: Just let me find the wrapper.

CAITLIN: *(Starts quickly looking for and putting on her clothes.)* I really really need to get to my pharmacy to get some more Ambien, Klonopin and the fucking Morning-After Pill.

STEVE: Yea, see, the thing is the whole city is on lock down.

CAITLIN: FUCK! They gotta let me at least go to the pharmacy?

STEVE: Even if you got there it would be closed.

CAITLIN: What a nightmare fucking week topped off by me catching an STD from Stan, some douche Yankee fan.

◎:10

STEVE: Steve.

CAITLIN: What?

STEVE: My name is Steve.

CAITLIN: Who gives a shit what your fucking name is!

STEVE: Caitlin, please calm down.

CAITLIN: I just wanna go home, and be under the sheets and for my fucking life just to be back to normal- That's it! Is that too much to ask?!

STEVE: Here, please! Have my vitaminwater!

CAITLIN: What?!

STEVE: You can't go outside, it's dangerous! Please, just drink the vitamin water. It will help with your hangover.

(CAITLIN *seems overwhelmed by the absurdity of the situation and plops down on the floor in front of the TV. Takes the vitamin water and guzzles it down while* STEVE *frantically searches apartment for any evidence of there having been safe sex that night.*)

STEVE: I never ever have sex without protection, it's just, if you gimme a minute to find the... YES!

CAITLIN: What?

STEVE: *(Finds the wrapper.)* I got it! *(Hands wrapper to* CAITLIN.*)*

CAITLIN: *(Reading.)* Rough Rider, ribbed for her pleasure.

STEVE: Yea, I think I just grabbed whatever they...

CAITLIN: Fine.

STEVE: I just, I hope now you can put your mind at ease.

CAITLIN: My mind at ease? It's never gonna be the same again. Ever. Not after this. *(Indicates the TV.)* Not Ever. Patriots' Day was my favorite holiday as a kid. I loved thinking, wow- every other kid in America had to go to school on Patriots' Day, but not us... Boston was extra super special... now, my city- what the fuck are we? I have all this shit inside me- I can't get it out of my head- that kid with both his legs gone, the man in the cowboy hat carrying him, its just so-/

STEVE: /I know

CAITLIN: That kid's face- he's so confused and scared and I just wanted to forget it happened, just for a few minutes, just for a few fucking minutes but it's everywhere, the TV, the radio, Facebook- no escape! I can't sleep- when I close my eyes I have this recurring nightmare about my legs getting blown off... Wait, you said before- They got one of 'em? Killed him on this block?

STEVE: Next block.

CAITLIN: *(Three separate thoughts in her head, one for each of these lines.)* Good. Assholes. I hope they fucking suffer. A lot.

STEVE: I'm sure they'll lift this curfew soon. Every police department in New England and the FBI and ATF and about a thousand K-9 units are hunting him.

CAITLIN: I had a German Shepherd as kid.

STEVE: His name was Buddy.

CAITLIN: Yea, he had the biggest nose for trouble you ever- wait, how did you know about Buddy?

STEVE: You told me at the bar last night.

CAITLIN: Really?

STEVE: We were talking about all the bomb-sniffing dogs around town and the good thing about that was they reminded you about Buddy and you knew that Buddy would always keep you safe.

CAITLIN: I don't talk about him with just anyone you know. I must've really liked you at the bar.

STEVE: You did come home with me.

CAITLIN: Yea... but, normally I'm not the best judge of character in those situations.

STEVE: I normally don't go out that much, actually. I bury myself in here with my books and my Netflix. Then something like this week happens. So I forced myself out of my comfort zone. Cause there is still the very best of humanity in many people.

CAITLIN: You thought you'd find the best in humanity at O'Malley's during two-for-one shot night?

STEVE: See... Under normal circumstances I wouldn't have gone to the bar, and under no circumstances would I have ever gone up to speak to you. So when I say I don't "normally" do this- the truth is I never do stuff like this.

(Tender moment between them. Then CAITLIN suddenly bolts up.)

CAITLIN: I remember why my shoulder hurts! I jumped out of bed naked and ran to the window to check out the noise and then there was that really big explosion and I felt you pull me down and get on top of me.

STEVE: Sorry about your shoulder- I should get you some Tylenol or Aleve? Which is better for your stomach?

CAITLIN: You threw me down then used your body as a shield to protect me.

STEVE: Um, I was just really reacting to, a- the...

CAITLIN: Then you checked to see if I was okay and put me back in bed, covered me with blankets, and you talked to calm me down. I told you dogs made me feel safe so you just kept naming as many hero dogs as you could remember, like Lassie and Scooby-Doo, and kept going 'til I finally passed out.

STEVE: It was an intense night.

(He offers her the Tylenol/Aleve. She takes the bottle, holding it.)

CAITLIN: Thank you.

STEVE: You don't have to thank me.

CAITLIN: You don't understand. I've dated assholes who wouldn't hold a door open for me let alone risk their lives with bombs and shit going off. We should definitely, like, ya know, hang out.

STEVE: Yea.

CAITLIN: I mean not just right now because we're stuck inside and could get shot if we go out on the street- but after- When we like have an actual choice about it?

STEVE: I'd love that. *(Doing his best impression of her accent.)* Sure.

CAITLIN: Wanna share this blanket with me?

(STEVE at first is tentative and awkward getting under the blanket and finding a comfortable position with CAITLIN- difficult because this is real and they are doing it sober, but this only lasts for a brief moment. They find it comfortable and natural under the blanket and their bodies fit together like it's the most natural thing in the world for them to be together here, right now- because it is. CAITLIN rests her head on STEVE and a peace and comfort register on her face like she hasn't felt in her life. STEVE is holding her like the protector he was last night and still is, as lights go to black.)

END OF PLAY

Shadow Saint
by Mark Borkowski

8

SHADOW SAINT by Mark Borkowski was first produced as part of Program B in Collective:10 at Teatro Círculo in New York City, and premiered October 9, 2014. It was directed by Karen Chamberlain. The cast was as follows:

BEA	Wendi Joy Franklin
RUDY	Khalil Muhammad

CHARACTERS
(in order of appearance)

RUDY: 30's

BEA: 60's. Rudy's mother.

SETTING

A living room in Brooklyn.

TIME

Present.

(At rise, RUDY sits at a table wearing a thousand-yard stare. BEA, his mother, roams about, cleaning the room.)

BEA: What're ya thinkin' about?

RUDY: Nothin'.

BEA: Nobody's ever thinkin' nothin'. We're always thinkin' about somethin'. I put ya clean clothes away. Ya hear me? *(Beat.)* You were out all night again. What a life. Sleep all day, out all night. You keep very strange hours. *(Beat.)* Ya know Gavatski's closin' 'is butcher shop today. For permanent. After forty-five years. I can't believe it's actually happening. I 'member the day he opened. The last of the ol' time butchers. Say goodbye to fresh Kielbasy. *(To herself.)* Where did my neighborhood go? Where has everybody gone? I walk these streets and I don't know anybody anymore. I used to know everybody. Everybody knew everybody. Now I'm a stranger. *(Beat. To Rudy.)* What d'ya do out there all night? Better watch it, ya get yaself hurt.

RUDY: Ya can't hurt the dead.

BEA: What was 'at?

RUDY: I'm dead, Ma.

BEA: Dead? You ain't dead! You're very much alive.

RUDY: I walk through the streets. Through the people. Through the dark. Their "night." That's what they call the darkness.

BEA: What d'ya mean ya walk through people?

RUDY: I'm a ghost, Ma. Nobody sees me anymore.

BEA: They see ya.

RUDY: No they don't.

BEA: Just cause they don't look at ya don't mean your not there.

RUDY: They don't see ghosts.

BEA: I see ya. It's all in your head. Ya spend too much time alone, isolatin' like ya do. It ain't natural, young guy like you. And ya ain't dead. Ya just... lonely, at's all. Loneliness is havin' a go at ya. Believe me, I know. After ya father passed on, I fell into it.

RUDY: Ya felt dead?

BEA: It was worse than dead. Loneliness that bad is worse than death. Ya can't let me live through that again.

RUDY: Live through what?

BEA: I saw what's inside your drawer.

RUDY: What's inside my drawer?

BEA: Under your shorts?

RUDY: Wait a minute-- what're ya doin' in my drawers?

BEA: Who washes ya filthy clothes and leaves 'em by ya door?

RUDY: What're ya even doin' in my room?!

BEA: They been layin' by ya door for a week. I was afraid the cats'd pee on 'em again. I saw the door was open so I--

RUDY: My door is never open! Stay out of my room!!

BEA: It ain't your room, and it ain't your door! It's my room, my door-- 'cause it's in my house!

RUDY: Will ya stop already!

BEA: What business you have with a gun?!

RUDY: You have a door, a room, a house and me, I have a gun!

BEA: Yeah, that's in my house! Get rid of it! Your father never had a gun in this house!

RUDY: Maybe if he did he wouldn't have hung himself.

BEA: Oh my God! Oh my God!!

RUDY: Ma, I'm sorry. I didn't mean to say that--

(He goes to hug her and she viciously whips him with a towel over and over--)

○):10

BEA: You cruel bastard you, how could ya talk about ya father like that, you wanna kill me, ya ungrateful son of a bitch!

RUDY: I'm sorry, Ma! Stop it! I think out loud, you-- ya know I do, I can't help it! I think out loud! Stop!!

BEA: Is that what it's for? My gonna find ya like *(Gasps.)* --like him? Is 'at it? Like father, like son?

RUDY: Ma, trust me, I'm not gonna kill myself. Besides, ya can't kill what's already dead.

BEA: And all this morbid talk. You're takin' drugs again.

RUDY: If I was takin' drugs, Ma, you'd know it, believe me.

BEA: What are ya doin' out there, ya robbin' people?

RUDY: No.

BEA: Sweet Jesus, I keep tellin' 'im to go to church. I tell 'im, "all good things happen when ya go to church."

RUDY: I went to church.

BEA: Bullshit!

RUDY: The other night. I couldn't get in. The doors were locked.

BEA: People break in!

RUDY: They lock up the "House of God"?!

BEA: They have to! The parish just got a huge twenty foot gold cross, covered with jewels.

RUDY: Did they forget the Lord's cross was made of wood?

BEA: I'm gonna call the cops on your ass! 'at's what I'm gonna do. I'll be damned if I'm gonna get a phone call you're dead. Then what?! What's gonna happen to me? I'll be hopeless. Rosie Nichols says, "Beatrice, ya don't know what hopeless means 'til ya lose a child." She lost her son Jimmy, now look at 'er. She's walkin' around, lookin' like a zombie.

RUDY: Don't compare me wit Jimmy Nichols.

BEA: Cryin' in the schoolyard late at night, callin' 'is name.

RUDY: Jimmy was a criminal, Ma.

BEA: How many times I go out in the middle o' the night and take her home?

RUDY: Criminals get shot, Ma.

BEA: What, you ain't a criminal? Your robbin' people!

RUDY: I am not!

BEA: They're gonna find ya dead somewhere. 'member them nightmares I used to have? 'bout you bein' found dead, under the highway?

RUDY: 'at's when I was on drugs.

BEA: That sheet over your body.

RUDY: I ain't on drugs no more, Ma.

BEA: Sweet Lord, he ain't suppose to be worryin' me like this, not at my age. He's supposed to be takin' care o' me!

RUDY: I do take care o' ya, Ma! Who runs your errands? Who takes ya to the leg doctor? Who?!

BEA: And who helps himself to my Social Security money?!

RUDY: What?! My God, 'at ain't happened for years!

RUDY: Take that back, Ma? Please? Take back what ya just said! Ya know it ain't true!

BEA: Think I need you, ya son of a bitch?! I need you like I need a whole in the head!

RUDY: It scrapes my insides ya say that shit to me! Ya talk about the past like it was yesterday. I go outta my way to make up for the past, to be a good son! You know I changed! Now take it back!

BEA: Get rid o' that gun!

RUDY: Why?

BEA: 'cause I said so!

RUDY: A gun is only dangerous if it has bullets in it.

BEA: Get rid o' the bullets too.

RUDY: There are no bullets.

BEA: Bullshit! What kind o' gun ain't got no bullets? Ya ever shoot anybody?

RUDY: It's never loaded. How my gonna shoot somebody if the gun's never loaded?

BEA: Your gonna get yaself killed. Then I'm gonna be all alone.

RUDY: Don't start, Ma.

BEA: All my life I gave and gave and gave! And for what?! To to be left alone in the end?! With nothin'!

RUDY: You don't get it, Ma. I'm one of the shadows.

○):10

BEA: You ain't no shadow!

RUDY: Yes I am!

BEA: --Stop talkin' crazy--

RUDY: --I'm a shadow--

BEA: You are not a shadow! YOU ARE MY SON!!

(She feels faint, nearly collapses. He hurries to her and walks her to a chair. She sits and breathes. Beat.)

BEA: I hate the past. *(Beat.)* What're ya doin' out there, Rudy?

RUDY: I... wait.

BEA: You wait? Okay. For what?

RUDY: For people to pass. Certain people. People who look a particular way. People who look like they need something.

BEA: "Need something?" What could they possibly need from you?

RUDY: And then I put my gun to their head. I step out of the dark and aim it at their skull.

BEA: Sweet Jesus.

RUDY: And... I watch them. I watch them fall completely apart. Slowly painfully fall completely apart. I don't hurt them. I don't even speak to them. I just watch them. Watch them beg.

BEA: They beg, the poor things?

RUDY: Oh, yeah, they beg-- they plead for mercy! The sweat that pours down their face. Tears mixing with the sweat. Body's tight, scared to death. Scared OF death. After a bit I cock back the hammer.

BEA: *(Gasps.)* Oh God.

RUDY: A click in the night. To them, the loudest sound they ever heard. Knees shaking, ready to kneel on the ground and beg. Mouths locked, words forget how to form. All their money, their gold, their fine houses-- it's all worthless-- I can have it all if I desired. But I don't. They would sell their very soul to me. That's right-- they would denounce the name of God! Just to live. What good is life once you've bargained your soul?

BEA: They denounce God? Ya must do somethin' terrible to make--

RUDY: No, no-- I never hurt anybody! I swear on Daddy's grave. Ever. I mean, the gun's not even loaded-- I never even bought bullets. And I have no intentions of ever killing. See, I give these people something. After it's over and I let them go, I feel like I've given them something very special.

BEA: Special?!

RUDY: The memory of that night-- the reality of that night will live in their brains forever. The fear, Ma, the ultimate fear has been faced. The worst is over for them. I really believe that. From that night on they live!

(Beat.)

BEA: This is what you do at night? And ya call that "giving?" You ain't givin', you're takin'!

RUDY: What am I takin'? I don't rob 'em!

BEA: Ya get people to "bargain their souls" and 'at ain't takin' somethin'? They "denounce the name of God" and 'at ain't robbin' people?

RUDY: I didn't think you'd understand.

BEA: I understand my son likes to torment people. What is it ya like about it? Seein' 'em on their knees? Hearin' 'em beg?

RUDY: How 'bout waking them up!

BEA: What are you, God's alarm clock? Ya used to be afraid o' the dark when you was a kid. Now... ya like livin' inside of it.

RUDY: I never said I liked it. I got no choice, Ma.

BEA: You can gimme the gun. *(No response. Beat.)* So I guess you're goin' out again tonight?

RUDY: Not tonight.

BEA: What, tonight's ya night off or somethin'?

RUDY: I feel like stayin' home tonight. With you.

BEA: *(Beat.)* Ya do?

RUDY: You're goin' to Gavatski's, right? Get us some o' that fresh Kielbasy.

BEA: Yes I am. If I ever get over there. Christ, look at the time! He's closin' his shop for good in... *(Beat, suspicious.)* Ya really gonna stay home tonight?

RUDY: Just you and me, Ma.

BEA: I'll be back in a half hour. *(She puts on her coat. Beat.)* Rudy?

RUDY: Yeah, Ma?

BEA: You ain't dead, son.

RUDY: Thanks, Ma.

◎):10

(BEA exits. RUDY *remains. After a moment,* RUDY *takes out the gun and places it on the table. He stares at it as lights fade to black.)*

END OF PLAY

END OF PLAY

Casey229
by Elin Hampton

4

CASEY229 by Elin Hampton was first produced as part of Program B in Collective:10 at Teatro Círculo in New York City, and premiered October 9, 2014. It was directed by Margaret Champagne. The cast was as follows:

KENTON CHESTER   John Norwell

PAM   Karen Chamberlain

CHARACTERS
(in order of appearance)

KENTON CHESTER: An overweight, middle-aged, balding man. He wears a T-shirt and sweatpants.

PAM: An attractive well-dressed woman, slightly past child-bearing age.

SETTING

A few miles from a better neighborhood.

TIME

A hot summer afternoon.

(Two garden chairs sit on the front porch of what charitably would be called a "humble house." KENTON CHESTER/CASEY, an out-of-shape schlump, sits on one of them. He wears a T-shirt from a previous weight, sweats, slippers, tiny sun shades, and earbuds. He listens to his iPod. PAM, an impeccably well-dressed woman in business attire, approaches him. She checks out the neighborhood with judgment, and looks at her phone, making sure the address is correct. She clears her throat.)

PAM: Hello? Is this 1017 South Andover?

CASEY: *(He jumps.)* I didn't expect you 'til tomorrow.

PAM: What?

CASEY: But everything's ready to go. Lemme put some shoes on. I can help you to the car. The wheelchair's kinda cumbersome.

PAM: No, I'm not here for a wheel--

CASEY: Oh, just her clothes. Sure. I'm an idiot. Goodwill wouldn't send a lady-- a lady in *heels* to get her equipment. Mom was seventy pounds at the end. Her stuff weighs about three times that.

PAM: Omigod. No, I'm not here to pick up-- I'm really sorry for you and your loss.

CASEY: Thanks. It was a long time coming. But you're never really prepared.

PAM: I imagine that's true. Um, I'm actually looking for someone. Your daughter, maybe?

CASEY: My daughter?

PAM: Or, I don't know, sister? A young woman. I know she lives here.

CASEY: There's no young woman here.

PAM: I know for a fact there is. The detective I hired tracked down her IP address.

CASEY: Detective? What the hell--

PAM: I regret the timing, I do, with your mom and all, but ever since I found out, I've been sick. Literally. Lost five pounds in two days. Shit, that was insensitive! You just told me about your mother withering away, and here I am blabbering about five pounds.

CASEY: You look fi--

PAM: *(Rambling.)* But I was completely blind-sided by this... Frank and I have been together for almost twenty years... I thought I was an intelligent person, but the truth is, I didn't have a clue... a mid-life crisis, really? I assumed he'd be above all that.

CASEY: Who ARE you?

PAM: Pam. Frank's wife. I know this is a terrible time for you and it's not your fault, of course. Frank's still attractive and charming. I guess he needed reassurance from some young hottie or whatever. Look, I'm not trying to cause a scene, I just want this to stop. So tell the whore who's living here to leave Frank alone!

CASEY: Who's Frank?

PAM: My husband. Frank, or *MeUnderscoreButch*... whatever the hell he's calling himself these days. He left his laptop opened, with a picture of her. Any psychiatrist would tell you, he wanted me to find out.

CASEY: *(Sinks into a chair. The wind has been knocked out of him.)* Butch is married?

PAM: Yes. I mean, Frank. There is no Butch. I'm Frank's wife. So you understand. I need to speak with Casey. Or as my husband lovingly calls her... *Casey229*.

CASEY: *(He shakes his head and self-consciously pulls his shirt over his gut.)* I'm Casey.

PAM: I've read the e mails! Casey's some slut. Excuse me. I don't mean to be calling your daughter names. I'm begging you, Mr.--

CASEY: Chester. Kenton Chester. KC. Casey. 229. Leap Day. It's a shitty birthday.

PAM: *(Shakes her head, trying to make sense of all of this.)* Then, who's the blonde in the photo?

CASEY: I don't know. I got her picture off ChristianMingle.com

PAM: *(She stares at him in disbelief.)* You're my husband's mistress?!

CASEY: No. It's not like that. Please don't trivialize it. Like it's something sordid and cheap. What *Casey229* and *MeUnderscoreButch* have is special.

PAM: Special. With you.

CASEY: With *Casey229*. It's a relationship. God, I'm so confused.

PAM: You're confused?! So, you're telling me my husband's, what, gay?!

CASEY: You'd know better than me. Butch and me... we've never met face to face. It didn't seem important.

PAM: So you're gay, and--

CASEY: No! I'm straight. First time we chatted, I assumed *MeUnderscoreButch* was a lesbian. I like lesbians. What guy would call himself Butch? Now, I think it's kinda cute. I saw what he was going for. I was just looking for someone to talk to... a friend. I don't expect you to understand.

PAM: You got that right.

CASEY: Hey. You're not the only one who's hurting here, Pamela.

PAM: Pam. Just, Pam.

CASEY: Pam. You don't know how lonely it can be, taking care of your mom for six years. After the amputation, she needed full-time help. Now you're probably thinking, "Why didn't he hire someone?"

PAM: Actually, I wasn't--

CASEY: And the answer is, I did. The first nurse just watched those so-called "reality" shows all day. The next one was crazy. She stole my mother's prosthetic leg and pawned it. I had to be the one... the one to take care of her. I'm an only child.

PAM: A nursing home might have been a good option.

CASEY: Move a houseful of memories into a one hundred fifty square foot room? I don't think so, Pam. I owed it to my mom to be there for her.

PAM: I'm still not understanding.

CASEY: It's not so easy to have a great social life when you spend most of your adult years housebound with your mother. Her disability check was enough for the two of us to get by, but there wasn't a whole lot left over to wine and dine the ladies, if you get my drift.

PAM: Okay. But where did Frank, Butch come into all of this?

CASEY: I'm getting to it. Here I am, pretty much in the dark about, you know, taking care of my eighty-seven-year-old-one-legged-mother. Not as easy as you'd think. So, I sign up for an online course to teach me the basics of home nursing care. Boy, when you sign up for anything on the Internet, suddenly you're on the list for like everything else out there. So this one day, I'm eating lunch. Onion soup *au gratin* and right at that instant, some school sends me a link about learning French. I wasn't looking to take a French class, but it's like when you go grocery shopping and you're about to leave and then you see a candy bar in the checkout line and you just can't pass it up.

PAM: Impulse buying.

CASEY: Right. That's what it was. So, I signed up. Did you know "*au gratin*" means with cheese?

PAM: Yes.

CASEY: Well I didn't. But, I do now. Then, coupla months later, I joined French Chat, y'know, to practice speaking all the words with other people.

PAM: And you met Frank... there?

CASEY: I met Butch.

PAM: Frank is fluent in French. He's originally from Quebec.

CASEY: She definitely impressed me. I mean, he. So Butch and me start talking and before we know it, we're just speaking in English. And by the time I realize he's a guy and he thinks I'm a girl, we're already, I don't know, connected. Really connected. A first for me. Never had that with anyone, not unless you count my mother, who sometimes put her arms around my neck, probably for support, but I kept telling myself it was a hug.

PAM: O-oh.

CASEY: I know. Pathetic, right? I'm telling you, if it hadn't been for Butch, there woulda been days I couldn'ta gotten outta bed. He's the one that kept me going.

PAM: *(She is moved. She touches his arm.)* That's so sweet.

CASEY: It was really romantic. I'm telling you what, life doesn't turn out like you plan it. *C'est la vie.* After about a year, he proposed... and I said "yes."

PAM: *(Pulls her hand back.)* You're married?!

CASEY: Going on two wonderful years.

PAM: This is insane.

CASEY: Love is insane, Pam.

PAM: So... you two have this idyllic marriage. Of course, you do. It's online. Well, Frank and I live in the real world! Our marriage may not be perfect, but it's REAL.

CASEY: Oh, ours is real. And I'm not going to lie to you, Pam, it hasn't been without its ups and downs either. Online marriage counseling really helped. We thought it was important for the kids to see us as a strong unit.

PAM: Kids?!

CASEY: Oh, yeah. I can see where that would come as a shock. When Butch and *Casey229* met, I was single mom.

©:10

PAM: Oh, Jesus.

CASEY: I know. I know. I got carried away. *SassyKira*'s twenty now. She's technically an adult, but she still needs, you know, guidance. Butch gets that. I wouldn't have married him if he hadn't been so great with Kira. He is a really good father.

PAM: We don't have any children.

CASEY: Huh. We talked about having a kid of our own, but after my hysterectomy...

PAM: O-mi-god.

CASEY: Butch was so understanding. He told *Casey229*, "There are so many kids in this great big world without parents. Why don't we adopt?" He was right. He always is. Someday, we'll help *MontegoRV* look for his virtual birth parents, but for now, we think it's best not to confuse him.

PAM: Montego.

CASEY: RV. Our son. Many guys would've been afraid to adopt an Ethiopian special needs child, but Butch knew how he was in even more in need of love. He was right again. Monte's had trouble making friends. Kids can be so nasty. That's why we got *PrettyPoodleSimon*. Thank God for dogs. They just love you all day long.

PAM: Never had one.

CASEY: It'll break my heart if we have to put him down. The vet said he can last another year or two if we keep with the gluten free diet. We do what we have to do. And Montego needs one more surgery. For his cleft palate.

PAM: Expensive kid.

CASEY: Whatever he needs. We're his parents and we love him.

PAM: Of course you do. Yes. How callous of me.

CASEY: The surgery isn't cheap, and insurance might not cover it, but Butch always provides for us, even if he has to work seven days a week to make ends meet. Thank God everyone needs a plumber!

PAM: Plumber? Frank's not a plumber!

CASEY: It's an honest living, Pamela. He didn't get to go to college.

PAM: But Frank went to Princeton. He was at the top of our class. That's where we met. I studied international law. Frank had a double major... philosophy and romance languages.

CASEY: High achievers. Boy, oh boy.

PAM: In hindsight, perhaps they weren't the most practical choices for him. Anyway, it turned out okay. Frank's career didn't work out, but now he works for me. At my law firm.

CASEY: He's a lawyer!

PAM: No, he's my assistant. He's a paralegal.

CASEY: Look at you, pretty and smart. You've got it all.

PAM: Right? I thought we did. It's a good life. We have a beautiful apartment with a doorman and a view, we eat in restaurants, we make charitable contributions, we take vacations. Spontaneously!

CASEY: So, no complaints.

PAM: Well, everyone has complaints. It's just that it doesn't sound like your life with Butch is an improvement over what Frank has with me. Am I missing something? From what you've told me, it seems as though you and Butch have a life riddled with problems.

CASEY: Challenges. We call 'em challenges. It's all how you look at it, I guess.

PAM: Frank and I decided long ago we didn't want children or pets. We wanted to be free.

CASEY: And so you are. *(Struggling.)* Look, I didn't know about you, Pam. I just wanted to make Butch as happy as he made me. God knows I liked being taken care of, for once in my life. But now that I know, I'm gonna break it off. It's what's right.

PAM: Yes. Good. *(She starts to leave, then stops and turns around.)* No. Give Butch another chance. He's doing the best he can.

CASEY: You sure?

(PAM walks back and hugs CASEY. He awkwardly accepts it.)

CASEY (CONT'D): This is a hug, right?

PAM: Yes. And thank you.

(She leaves. CASEY watches her go.)

CASEY: *Adieu.*

(Fade to black.)

END OF PLAY

○ :10

Uncle Silas
by Sayra Player

10

UNCLE SILAS by Sayra Player was first produced as part of Program B in Collective:10 at Teatro Círculo in New York City, and premiered October 9, 2014. It was directed by Sayra Player. The cast was as follows:

MAUREEN	Booker Garrett
SILAS	Kevin Kane

CHARACTERS
(in order of appearance)

MAUREEN: A wild-haired woman wearing an oversized T-shirt.

SILAS: Her brother.

SETTING

A studio apartment.

(The song 'I'll Take Care Of U' by Gil Scott-Heron and Jamie xx plays. MAUREEN *enters with a tiny newborn and lies on her side to nurse. All throughout the play* MAUREEN *is in a lot of pain, the only thing keeping her from passing out is adrenaline and the high she has from her body's natural painkillers.)*

MAUREEN: There you go. You got it. You got it. *(Shudders.)* Holy Christ. *(She takes a long exhale, to overcome the pain. Her glass of water is just out of reach. No matter how she tries she can't get it without removing her nipple.)*

(Lights come up, music fades. We hear the sound of her door buzzer.)

MAUREEN (CONT'D): *(She maneuvers her broken body to the door, holding the tiny baby, still attached to her breast.)* Yes?

SILAS: Hey, Mo.

*(*MAUREEN *is shocked and unsure what to do.)*

SILAS (CONT'D): Hello? These bags are about to break.

(She tentatively opens the door. SILAS *looks like a wet homeless guy, he carries balloons, a backpack, a grocery bag and a slice of pizza. He has a peaceful hopelessness about him.)*

SILAS (CONT'D): Oh. My. God. My little Mo is a mommy. Look at...

MAUREEN: Grab a towel from that pile and take off your shoes. *(Beat.)* When did you get in town?

SILAS: *(Hustling to put down all the stuff, get his shoes off so he can take a good look at the baby.)* I just got here. It's like a sauna in here. Should we, should I not talk? Is she awake?

MAUREEN: She's been nursing for six hours straight, feels like someone's sawing my nipples off. I gotta figure out how to get my nipple out of there. *(She works on getting nipple out and baby down.)*

(SILAS takes a bite of his pizza, but doesn't want it after all.)

MAUREEN (CONT'D): *(Resists yelling at him.)* Where are you staying?

SILAS: The Peninsula.

MAUREEN: Sounds fancy.

SILAS: Midtown, but they have an indoor pool with a bar. You'd love it.

MAUREEN: How long?

SILAS: A while, you can come swim when you feel better.

MAUREEN: You're a pig.

SILAS: *(Dries his head with the towel in resignation.)* Sure.

MAUREEN: Ditching your family... to do... God knows what, in some expensive hotel, I'm not swimming there, I'm a little busy.

SILAS: Mel and Leroy are set up, they won't need anything for a couple hundred years.

(MAUREEN glares at him.)

SILAS (CONT'D): I'm gonna go back. Anyway I'm here to see you and this baby. Can we not talk about my life?

MAUREEN: I know she kicked you out.

SILAS: I never said she didn't, come on I just want to celebrate the baby, not-

MAUREEN: And acting like you will have me over for a swim? How hard was it for you to come here today?

(Beat.)

SILAS: Hard.

MAUREEN: You're not really even here to see me. You came to lock yourself up in that hotel room.

SILAS: What does that mean? I'm here. I'm gonna stay and get some work done, I can come help you out anytime-

MAUREEN: You're writing? How's that going?

SILAS: *(Apathetically.)* My agent says the best of my career.

MAUREEN: You realize you're making everyone who loves you miserable. I think about you and my blood rages around in my veins like ball bearings. I'm supposed to stay calm... I need to create a good home for my baby. *(Beat.)* I can't have you here, Silas.

SILAS: You don't need to be so angry.

MAUREEN: It affects me. This affects all of us.

SILAS: I'm sorry. *(Beat.)* I brought you food. You need food. Almonds and healthy things. I have a couple of packs of cupcakes for me, but if you want them, I'm happy to-

MAUREEN: Gimme a cupcake. *(She takes a cupcake.)* You look dirty.

SILAS: Ah! I forgot to change. Can I change? So I can hold her. *(Points to restroom.)* In here?

MAUREEN: You're not holding her.

(He grabs his backpack.)

MAUREEN (CONT'D): Leave your bag.

(She locks eyes with him.)

MAUREEN (CONT'D): You're not going in there with that bag.

(He grabs a shirt and pants out of his bag. She watches him closely.)

SILAS: Be nice to have a picture of her with her uncle Silas, right?

(Nothing. He goes into the restroom. MAUREEN waits a few seconds and carefully goes through his big backpack, until she pulls out a milk carton, dumps it on the table. There are hypodermic needles, fifty wax paper squares of yellow powder in bundles, pills and marijuana.)

SILAS: *(Offstage.)* Ma said you did it here! That's so impressive. I saw Melanie give birth and that was some crazy shit with painkillers. Did you do it in the tub here? Did she come out in here? Mo? Wait, here I come.

(SILAS comes out, sees his drugs on the table and MAUREEN reading pill bottles.)

SILAS: Yep, yep, yep, I thought maybe you'd do that... now what?

MAUREEN: *(Throws a handful at him.)* Get rid of it! Get it out of here! Why do I let you people in here?

SILAS: *(Gets down on the floor, packs it all up in his backpack.)* I'm sorry, Mo. I'm gonna go.

MAUREEN: Why did you bring it here?

SILAS: I picked it up on my way here. I'm gonna just go check into the hotel and...

MAUREEN: What is wrong with you? Why is there so much?

(No answer.)

MAUREEN (CONT'D): Really. There's enough for a hundred people.

SILAS: I don't know. I didn't want to have to buy more? It's supposed to be really pure.

MAUREEN: I want to kill your doctor. Did he know you were clean for fifteen years. Did he assume because you're a big shot that you are dying to get high?

SILAS: You think that's why he gave me painkillers.

MAUREEN: You'd think you'd have a good doctor!!!

SILAS: I had surgery.

MAUREEN: That's bullshit. You know you can't take opiates! He knew too and he didn't care!

SILAS: He cared enough to stop giving 'em to me.

MAUREEN: Yeah?! And then what? I'm sick with this. I'm sick. *(She lays on her side.)*

SILAS: I'm sorry.

MAUREEN: What're you doing here? Rubbing it in my face? I just performed a miracle. I'm cohabitating with an angel. Can't I just be happy?

SILAS: Yes, be happy! I want that. Ma said you needed help so I came.

MAUREEN: I do need help!!! Where's Mom?! Hiding! Drinking. You guys are such pussies! She visited me once- once, the day after the birth- she sat there and drank an entire bottle of Prosecco and had me comfort her while she cried about you. I'm sick with it! And now you're here, in my face, looking so sorry. I don't have anymore to say. *(Pause.)* I don't want you to die, I don't want Leroy to not have his Papa.

SILAS: *(He goes to rub her back.)* Is this okay?

MAUREEN: I'm so broken, I'd let a homeless man massage me. Soft, like a flower petal.

SILAS: Are you okay?

MAUREEN: I feel... like... week-old roadkill that has just peeled itself off the highway. My arms hurt just laying here, yet they bend and hold a baby all day. My sacrum feels like someone crushed it with a hammer. I'm wearing a diaper because I'm bleeding something that smells like rotten meat, yes, it's disgusting. Silas, I have stitches on my vagina. There's no way your pain is worse than mine and I haven't even taken an aspirin. I want you to stay here with me. I want you to get clean. You can puke your brains out in my toilet, you can scream, holler, cry. The baby's not gonna care, it's the same thing she does all day.

(SILAS slipped into a nod sometime around "pain is worse than mine.")

MAUREEN (CONT'D): *(Stares for a bit and then gives him a nudge.)* You fell asleep.

SILAS: *(Bolting up.)* I wasn't asleep. I heard you.

MAUREEN: You got high in the bathroom.

SILAS: I'm barely high. I'm just sleepy. *(He leans over the baby.)* She looks so peaceful.

MAUREEN: Step back.

SILAS: You are going to love her so good, kid.

MAUREEN: Yes I am. Silas, you need to go to a hospital.

SILAS: *(Begins to wander around room, scratching his scruff.)* Can't.

MAUREEN: You're sick though, Silas. If you had a bone sticking out of your arm, would you go to the hospital?

SILAS: I don't have a bone problem. Hospitals are for bones. I have a need. The last thing I want is to hurt my family. You're asking this guy falling from the sky not to scream, and what you don't realize is the building was on fire. It is what it is. Look, let me hold your baby. I'm going to take some deep breaths and I'm going to fill my heart and mind with all the good and pure love in me, which there is a lot, and I'm gonna hold my first baby niece, and you are going to take a picture. *(He hands her his phone.)*

MAUREEN: *(She ignores as she comforts her baby.)* She is going to be treated like the baby Buddha. No harm will come her way. No suffering. I want you to hold her but you're high. I can't.

SILAS: There is no chance I will harm her in any way. None. I will sit here in the center of the bed. Nothing can go wrong. See. All bed. All soft. Now you just hand her to me. I promise.

(SILAS takes a few deep breaths. MAUREEN hands him the baby.)

SILAS (CONT'D): *(He takes in the baby's features.)* She's so little. Look at her eyelashes! Oh my heart, it's pounding, you're a lil' squish.

MAUREEN: Hey.

(MAUREEN holds up the camera, SILAS proudly smiles. A picture is taken.)

SILAS: *(As SILAS interacts with the baby, everything he is losing starts weighing on him and we see him begin to crack.)* She's opening her eyes. Whassup! Hi. Hi. Hi. I'm your uncle Silas, I'm your uncle Silas and I love you and your mommy very much... *(To MAUREEN.)* She's doing a mouth thing. I don't know- *(He trembles as he hands her the baby. SILAS grabs his backpack.)* I gotta go. Do you need to sit?

MAUREEN: Can't sit. I can only lay or stand.

SILAS: You need anything else before I go?

MAUREEN: I need my brother.

SILAS: I'm sending you the pic now. Call me anytime you need me. I have a lot of work to catch up on, but maybe I will come see you again next week.

MAUREEN: Don't go.

SILAS: I'll come back. Okay?

MAUREEN: *(Knowing she will probably never see him again.)* That would make me happy.

SILAS: Then I'm gonna do it!

MAUREEN: I love you.

SILAS: I love you.

(Door closes.)

(Blackout.)

END OF PLAY

Aunt Sylvia Is Dead
by Jenny Rachel Weiner

2

AUNT SYLVIA IS DEAD by Jenny Rachel Weiner was first produced as part of Program B in Collective:10 at Teatro Círculo in New York City, and premiered October 9, 2014. It was directed by Robert Z Grant and JB Roté. The cast was as follows:

CARRIE	Margaret Champagne
DIERDRE	Nina Mehta
FREDDY	Daniel O'Shea
JUNE	Naomi Warner
MALASSA	Sat Charn Fox
PAULA	Joan Porter
VAL	JB Roté

SETTING

A cramped hospital room in South Florida.

TIME

Late at night.

CHARACTERS
(in order of appearance)

DIERDRE: 40's. Female. A Reiki and yoga instructor at a wellness center; deeply angry but is working through it with her psychic; a proud lesbian who came out later in life.

VAL: 40's. Female. An office assistant who poses as a high powered attorney in familial situations; wears suits from Ross Dress For Less; has an active and secretive online dating life.

CARRIE: 40's. Female. The only niece who procreated; owns a moderately priced boutique that specializes in handmade birdhouses; easily stressed; the least financially stable of the bunch.

FREDDY: 50's/60's. Male. A power suit with a recreational cocaine habit; has never held onto a relationship; secretly loves cats and cries at Hallmark commercials.

PAULA: 60's. Female. The eldest niece of Aunt Sylvia; believes she is the Matriarch-in-training; collects Kathy comic strips and has a mug that reads "Leave me Alone! I'm Knitting!"

JUNE: 20's. Female. CARRIE'S daughter. Lost; occasionally catatonic, but only because she is paralyzed by fear of adulthood.

MALASSA: 30's. Female. Dierdre's partner; she is a hemp jewelry designer by trade and works at the green juice bar at a 24 Hour Fitness for money; rarely wears underwear or deodorant.

(Lights up on the hospital room. We meet the family: JUNE, wearing crusty clothes, zones out, staring at the muted TV. PAULA sits on the windowsill reading sympathy cards. FREDDY, VAL, CARRIE, and DIERDRE stand around AUNT SYLVIA, who is lying in a hospital bed hooked up to machines.)

DIERDRE: She looks so peaceful.

VAL: She's not. There are tubes up her nose.

DIERDRE: Don't snap at me.

VAL: I'm not snapping. AUNT SYLVIA IS DEAD!

DIERDRE: SHE'S NOT DEAD YET!

CARRIE: Don't diminish Dierdre's feelings, Val.

VAL: She's delusional!

DIERDRE: Haven't any of you ever heard of miracles?

FREDDY: Shut up, Dede. Nobody wants to hear your hippy dippy shit.

DIERDRE: Oh! He speaks! First thing you've said to me all day. Of course it's an insult. Why should I expect anything less.

FREDDY: Shh.

CARRIE: You can't fault her for being honest.

FREDDY: I'm not faulting anybody. I'm trying to grieve.

DIERDRE: You don't need to grieve yet! Nothing's happened!

FREDDY: Dierdre, why don't you go do some yoga in the visitor room. I'm sure all of the drug addicts are dying for some spiritual healing.

DIERDRE: Don't bully me right now, Freddy, do not.

FREDDY: Who's bullying? I'm trying to help you. I'm trying to share the wealth that is Dierdre.

CARRIE: Freddy.

VAL: Carrie, don't get involved.

CARRIE: Don't tell me what to do, Val! I'm defending my sister!

VAL: She's my sister, too!

PAULA: These cards are really very beautiful. Junebug, don't you think? June?

JUNE: Huh?

PAULA: Honey, quit watching television and come over here.

CARRIE: Paula, leave her alone. If she wants to watch television, let her.

PAULA: It's bad for her eyes.

CARRIE: Paula, mind your business and stop trying to parent my kid.

PAULA: Well, someone needs to!

CARRIE: Leave it, Paula!

PAULA: June, come here.

(PAULA tries to retrieve JUNE. JUNE resists.)

JUNE: NO!

PAULA: Come on!

(PAULA pulls at JUNE harder.)

JUNE: GET OFF ME, AUNT PAULA!	PAULA: You're acting like an imbecile!
JUNE: WHO SAYS IMBECILE ANYMORE?	PAULA: YOU ARE NEGLECTED! I AM TRYING TO GIVE YOU ATTENTION! Jesus, you smell like cottage cheese!
JUNE: That's because I ate that for breakfast! It's a perfectly reasonable thing to smell like! Mom!	

CARRIE: Both of you! Quit it. Aunt Sylvia is almost dead. Have some respect.

JUNE: Sorry.

PAULA: Junie, come here, Sweetie. Come look at what all the nice people are saying about Aunt Sylvia.

(JUNE goes over to PAULA.)

JUNE: *(She reads.)* "May God Be With You... Call upon me in the day of trouble, I will deliver thee..." Do they know we're Jewish?

PAULA: This card is from Aunt Sylvia's nail girl. I think it's from the dollar store across the street.

JUNE: Aw. That's sweet.

PAULA: She loved her very much. Aunt Sylvia always gave her a huge tip and a dried fruit basket on the holidays.

JUNE: "Some Blessings last for a short time, but some are called Aunts and enrich our lives...even after they're gone." That's depressing.

PAULA: This is the selection. Everyone is doing their best.

FREDDY: Val, who do we know here who can get us some weed?

VAL: I don't think I know anybody who still lives in Florida. Oh! There's that dude I used to screw from the deli.

FREDDY: Ooh, call him! You could probably also use a shtup, honey. Two for one?

VAL: I do not need some deli dick, Fred. I am a high powered attorney.

FREDDY: Call him, Val. We need something to get us through the night.

VAL: Can we do something about the lighting in here? These fluorescents are killing my eyes.

FREDDY: I'll call HR.

JUNE: Who do you think is going to get Aunt Sylvia's fur coat?

PAULA: I don't know, Sweetie. I don't think anyone is thinking about that right now

JUNE: Okay.

(Suddenly, MALASSA, Dierdre's partner, ushers herself in, beelining for DIERDRE.)

DIERDRE: Oh, thank God!

VAL: I'm glad someone's husband cares enough to make it here.

DIERDRE: Val.

VAL: You know what I mean. Hi, Malassa.

ALL: Hi, Malassa.

MALASSA: Hi, everybody. I'm really sorry for what's happening.

◎:10

FREDDY: *(Gets a whiff of* JUNE.*)* June, when's the last time you took off those filthy clothes? You're probably carrying disease.

CARRIE: Do not talk to my child like that, Freddy. Do not, do you hear me.

FREDDY: Hey, Carrie, how about taking the firecracker out of your cunt?

DIERDRE: *(To* MALASSA.*)* This is hell. I can't get a word in. My poor Aunt Sylvia is sitting here dying, and everyone is too busy being egomaniacs to just be here with her and help her heal.

MALASSA: Should we practice some Reiki on her?

DIERDRE: I'm so glad you're here.

*(*DIERDRE *and* MALASSA *start doing Reiki on* AUNT SYLVIA'S *body while* CARRIE *and* FREDDY *fight over* AUNT SYLVIA'S *body.)*

FREDDY: Someone needs to give this "child" a dose of reality! She's the only grand-niece, she's the one to carry on the tradition, and she's acting like a fucking idiot! The rest of us don't have the *luxury* of having children and yours is a poor excuse for a legacy. Look at her! She literally has toothpaste *in her ear.* Like, how does that happen? She's twenty-six and can barely do anything for herself. You coddle her and you expect her to go out and make a living on her own? You treat her like she's still in your womb!

CARRIE: I will not say this again. You do not know the first thing about being a parent, Freddy, all you know how to do is fuck prostitutes and give yourself a quick handjob in the pantry! You don't think I won't bring that up, it's alllll coming out today! That's for sure! Aunt Sylvia is dying, and there's nothing holding me back from *revealing* the truth of this family to whoever will listen! I am DONE PRETENDING do you hear me? I have a successful business, I am a *boutique owner,* and I have a wonderful, loving child, unlike the rest of you who couldn't get it together enough to make something of your lives. I am the one in charge here, don't you see? I am the ONLY one who has the capacity to handle this situation! *EMOTIONALLY.*

VAL: Wow.

PAULA: Carrie, I think you need to take a walk.

CARRIE: Me? What did I do? *He attacked me.*

DIERDRE: You know Aunt Sylvia loves our dogs like her own grandchildren. You know that.

CARRIE: When did I say anything about your dogs? Can we move on?

JUNE: I'm not ready to move on. Uncle Freddy, you just said some really mean shit about me.

DIERDRE: Is anyone listening to me? I'm trying to speak my truth here.

FREDDY: It was more directed at your mother than at you.

JUNE: Uh. OK.

FREDDY: You are very beautiful.

PAULA: Be careful. He likes 'em young.

(FREDDY slaps PAULA. JUNE disappears.)

VAL: ENOUGH! Tensions are high. This is not us. We are better than this. Our family is not *this family*. I don't want Aunt Sylvia to remember us like this.

CARRIE: Val's right. We love each other. That's why we're fighting! That's it! It's normal. Malassa, was it like this when your mother died last month?

DIERDRE: AUNT SYLVIA HASN'T DIED YET!

FREDDY: SHUT UP, DEDE.

DIERDRE: Why doesn't anybody listen to me in this family? It's like my beliefs don't matter, it's like my feelings are just pushed under the rug because I'm the youngest, because I am actually connected to my chakras, and because I'm a lesbian.

VAL: Honey, you are overreacting. We love that you're a lesbian.

PAULA: Aunt Sylvia?

CARRIE: She can't hear you, Paula.

DIERDRE: I don't believe you. *(Closes her eyes and starts to hum.)*

PAULA: Aunt Sylvia? Hi, it's Polly. I love you. I'm sorry you're suffering. Can you hear me? I'm sorry I haven't always been patient with you. I'm sorry I sometimes tell you my phone is breaking up when really I just can't stand hearing about your bridge game for another second.

PAULA (CONT'D): I love when you tell me I should wear blue eye shadow, that it brings out my eyes. Because my eyes are brown. I love that you call me Polly Pocket. I love that you sewed my name into all my underwear. I love that you give me kisses on my eyelids. I love that you always know the right time to bring out snacks. I promise, we will take care of each other. We will fiercely love each other, and we will pick each other up when we're down, and we will wipe the drool from each others' chins when our reflexes go. I love you. I love you, Aunt Sylvia. I promise we won't let you down.

DIERDRE: *(She sings.)* Stayed in bed all morning just to pass the time / There's something wrong here, there can be no denying / One of us is changing, or maybe we've stopped trying / And it's too late, baby, now it's too late / Though we really did try to make it / Something inside has died and I can't hide / And I just can't fake it / There'll be good times again for me and you / But we just can't stay together, don't you feel it, too / Still I'm glad for what we had, and how I once loved you

(AUNT SYLVIA starts to stir. She opens her eyes. Everybody gasps. AUNT SYLVIA gasps.)

◉:10

CARRIE: AUNT SYLVIA!

(AUNT SYLVIA stares at the ceiling. One drop of drool drips down her chin. All of the kids go to wipe it away. They let each other. JUNE comes out of the closet wearing all of AUNT SYLVIA'S clothes including her shoes, her wig and her fur coat. She wears heavy makeup and false teeth. She looks glamorous. All of the kids watch her as she struts around the room taking on the personality of AUNT SYLVIA. It's electrical and dynamic; theatrical and absurd.)

JUNE: *(As SYLVIA.)* Darlings, my time has come. You've been like my children all these years. When your parents died in that horrific accident, it was my duty and absolute pleasure to take you on as my own. And it has been the joy of my life to raise you up. So you can stand on mountains. And raise you up, to walk on stormy seas.

MALASSA: Is she quoting Josh Groban?

JUNE (CONT'D): *(As SYLVIA.)* I never asked for anything in return. I never found love, but that's okay. I never had my own biological children, but that's okay. I had you. And that was enough. I had you, I had my health, and I had my furs. Darlings, please. Please be good to each other. You're all you have. You're what counts. Do you hear me?

ALL: Yes, Aunt Sylvia!

JUNE: *(As SYLVIA.)* Good. Now leave me the fuck alone. I'd like to die in peace.

(The children all begin to shuffle out. They each give AUNT SYLVIA a kiss as they leave. In the end, only JUNE is left.)

JUNE: *(As SYLVIA.)* Goodbye, darling. Thanks for the mink. *(Places her hands over AUNT SYLVIA'S eyelids. Then exits.)*

(AUNT SYLVIA smiles.)

(Lights down.)

END OF PLAY

Park Slope Minstrel Show
by Eleanor Burgess

PARK SLOPE MINSTREL SHOW by Eleanor Burgess was selected from over one thousand blind submissions exclusively for publication as part of Collective:10.

CHARACTERS
(in order of appearance)

DYLAN: 30's. Male. White. Probably wearing a Yo La Tengo T-shirt.

MILES: Age 6. Annie and Dylan's son. Totally adorable.

FLANNERY: Age 8. Annie and Dylan's daughter. Smart as a whip.

ANNIE: 30's. Female. White. Probably wearing black.

SETTING

The ground floor living room of a Park Slope brownstone. An ottoman sits at the center of the room. If any furniture is possible besides the ottoman: bookcases.

(DYLAN and ANNIE *stand, looking down at* FLANNERY *and* MILES, *who sit on the ottoman.* FLANNERY *and* MILES *are adorable, curly-haired, Caucasian children, straight out of a paper towel commercial. Both of their faces are covered with black face paint.)*

DYLAN: Did anybody see you?

MILES: No.

FLANNERY: That's against the rules.

ANNIE: What, exactly, are the rules to the game "Harriet Tubman?"

FLANNERY: Well, the closet over there, is where they have the slaves locked up-

MILES: Under the stairs.

DYLAN: Jesus.

ANNIE: Uh huh.

FLANNERY: So you're there. And then Harriet Tubman comes, and breaks you out, and you both have to hide.

ANNIE: Oh - hear that, Dylan?

FLANNERY: And you want to work your way to the door, but you have to stay hidden, behind like the furniture, you can't be out in the open for more than two seconds, or they find you and-

MILES: It's the fugi - it's the fuge-

FLANNERY: And it's the fugitive slave law so they get you-

MILES: They get you.

FLANNERY: And you have to go back to the closet and start again.

ANNIE: Well, that is - impressively accurate.

DYLAN: Kids. Mommy and Daddy aren't angry. We really respect the creativity and thoughtfulness that you put into this game. And you know we support your expressing your creativity in an open ended way during play time. But - you can never ever play that game ever again. Ever.

FLANNERY: We were really careful not to get any face paint on the couch.

MILES: That's why we couldn't put any on our hands.

ANNIE: Thank you for that, that was really considerate.

FLANNERY: And that's why we kept - more than half the game is outside.

(Beat.)

DYLAN: Outside?

FLANNERY: Yeah. Cuz once you sneak out of the house you have to follow the North Star.

ANNIE: Where exactly is the North Star?

MILES: It's the brightest light in the sky!

ANNIE: You mean the sun?

FLANNERY: It's the mosquito thing.

ANNIE: The bug zapper?

FLANNERY: Yeah you follow that until you cross the border into Canada.

(This is bad news to ANNIE and DYLAN.)

DYLAN: Did - either of you guys make it to Canada?

MILES: We both did!

FLANNERY: Yeah I helped him escape and then he came back for his family. *(She holds up three stuffed animals, all of whose faces have been crudely painted black.)*

DYLAN: And you all went - over the fence?

FLANNERY: Across the border.

DYLAN: To Ms. Walker's place?

FLANNERY: To Canada, yeah.

MILES: That's how you win!

DYLAN: Oh God. Oh no.

ANNIE: It just had to be Deborah's yard, didn't it? It couldn't be Robin's yard. Or Jerry's. Deborah had to have a compost heap. So we had to have mosquitoes. So we had to have a mosquito zapper, right by the compost, right by Deborah's yard.

DYLAN: What do we do?

ANNIE: Run away to the real Canada?

DYLAN: *(Pulls up a chair near the kids, takes a seat.)* Flannery. Miles. Sometimes a game of dress-up is not just a game of dress-up. Playing Harriet Tubman is different from playing Luke and Leia. There are socio-historical factors. There are socio-cultural-historical factors...The game that you were playing could really hurt some people.

FLANNERY: But we didn't use the slingshots or anything.

DYLAN: It could remind them of something that is pretty upsetting.

MILES: Like Canada.

DYLAN: No, it reminds people of slavery, and that makes them sad.

FLANNERY: But then they escape from slavery. Like Passover.

DYLAN: You know, what I would really like to do, is - let's all find our shoes. We'll go next door, and go see Ms. Walker, and we'll just have a little chat with her-

ANNIE: Really, that's what you'd prefer to do - to apologize to Deborah? Before we've finished explaining anything to them?

DYLAN: I just think - you know - before she goes to bed-

ANNIE: It's five-

DYLAN: Or goes out-

ANNIE: Or talks to anyone else-

DYLAN: We'll just go across the yard, and ask if she has a little time to talk.

FLANNERY: I don't like Ms. Walker's place. It smells.

ANNIE: That would be the compost.

DYLAN: Look, it'll be easy. We'll just, take a little walk over there-

ANNIE: She'll offer us some gluten free brownies-

DYLAN: We'll sit down for maybe ten or fifteen/ minutes.

ANNIE: /forty-five minutes.

DYLAN: And we'll just talk a little bit.

ANNIE: If she asks you if you spend much time watching TV, what do you answer-

FLANNERY/MILES: *(Together.)* Only PBS.

ANNIE: Aww, they're so smart. Look at the smart kids we raised.

DYLAN: You'll just tell her some of the stuff we've been talking about here. You know, how you didn't know, but we've told you more now about the connotations of it, and you would never even consider doing it again.

FLANNERY: I don't think I will remember that.

DYLAN: Yeah, that's fine, Mom and I will be there, we'll all talk about it together-

ANNIE: She may introduce you to her partner, don't worry about it, that's just a fancy name for husband, that some people like to use, because they're full of it. Oh, and hey, if you guys want to slip in there, that you took turns being Harriet Tubman, and that- *(To MILES.)* You're the one who went back to rescue your family, I think we can recoup pretty much all of the points we've lost.

(Beat.)

DYLAN: Hey, guys, could you - ah - can you, ah, maybe go wash that stuff off? Flannery, can you help your brother?

FLANNERY: Sure.

DYLAN: Thank you, Flannery, We appreciate it.

(FLANNERY and MILES exit.)

ANNIE: You wanted to show them Ken Burns. "They're too young," I said. "They'll have nightmares." "No," you said, "it's time, they should face what it means to be an American, Howard Zinn is still a little too advanced for their reading level..."

(He doesn't say anything.)

ANNIE (CONT'D): I'm glad we got the organic face paints. I feel so much better about them doing all that crazy stuff when I know the only thing going into their pores is pulverized carob.

DYLAN: We agreed. We agreed, if it's always me that talks to them, about serious subjects - if you just make jokes about things, and I have to actually explain the rules, they'll develop these very gendered ideas-

ANNIE: Right.

DYLAN: -that men are always scary, or, or the last word on discipline, and that women are always nice.

ANNIE: No, I understand. That would be terrible.

DYLAN: You know all of - all of the studies show that sarcasm is the most damaging thing you can allow yourself to do, as a parent, or as a spouse.

ANNIE: I am not apologizing to Deborah. Oh come on, Dylan - Deborah? Deborah! The woman who thought I should breast feed Miles until he was five? Agree with me, here.

(No answer.)

ANNIE (CONT'D): It's not like she's even black or anything! It's not like we even have black neighbors!

DYLAN: Racism is everybody's problem.

ANNIE: I know. There are socio-historical cultural factors. I got a BA, too.

DYLAN: I built those compost heaps for Deborah. Which you know. *(Beat.)* And Deb actually eats gluten.

ANNIE: Fine, tempeh something whatever. Kale. Flavored local honey.

DYLAN: You did see me making gluten free cookies, for Flannery to take in on her birthday. Maybe that's what was kicking around in your memory.

ANNIE: Yeah, maybe that's it.

(They stare each other down.)

ANNIE: It's so sweet of you to do things like that. To handle the birthday baking. You must feel really good about yourself as a father. And how you were so careful, just now, to make sure they didn't feel guilty. You're so sensitive to everyone's feelings. I'm really going to enjoy the follow-up conversation where you find a sensitive and supportive way to tell our kids they're only allowed to dress up as white people.

DYLAN: I would never say that.

ANNIE: Remember that time, you wanted to sit them down and preemptively say, if you want to dress like a woman, if you want to dress like a man, we support you, that is 100% okay-

DYLAN: That is different, that is letting them be their true selves. You can't become black.

ANNIE: You can't become a woman either! I've got a riddle for you. A real logic puzzle. Right up there with whether God can make a rock so big he can't lift it. You ready?

DYLAN: I don't think we should have a conversation while you're in such a cruel and dismissive mood. *(He starts to go.)*

ANNIE: Why are drag queens okay and minstrel shows bad? Any chance the answer is because the people you like like one and the people you like don't like the other? And it would suck to have any of them dislike you. It would be the absolute worst to have anyone, ever, in the whole wide world, not acknowledge that you are the most bestest at being nice and fair of anybody ever-

DYLAN: You know you are being a real-

ANNIE: Bitch?

DYLAN: You are being a jerk. A mean-spirited-

ANNIE: Harpy?

DYLAN: -vicious-

ANNIE: Crazy?

DYLAN: -real shit of a person.

ANNIE: I'm just being honest. I think it's really important that we have an open line of communication in our marriage. That we both get to really feel heard.

DYLAN: Anything else you want to be honest about?

ANNIE: I'm pretty sure I'm okay with GMOs. I'm afraid of people with mental illnesses. I'm either afraid of them or I think they're wusses. I don't think "generalized anxiety" is mental illness, I think it's just being a wuss. I do think chopsticks are a really fucking silly way to eat food. I hate using them. Nothing is easier to eat with chopsticks than with a fork. Do you want to disagree with me?

DYLAN: I can't talk with you when you're like this.

ANNIE: I think I'd be a little unhappy if either Flannery or Miles turns out to be gay. I judge fat people. All the time. I think fat people should pay more for health insurance. If I have to give money to either Americans or foreigners I'd rather give money to Americans, I care more about them. I'm not sure I disagree with racial profiling. If I'd found out one of our kids was going to be born disabled, I would have had an abortion. I think - I think there was a time ten or so years ago when you might have agreed with me. Or you might have at least entertained the idea. We might have had a debate about it. You might have been able to change my mind. You might have actually had enough reasons to change my mind. When did you stop thinking, Dylan? When did you stop thinking? When did you lose all grasp on honesty? Or on original thought? You gutless cunt!

(He slaps her. Once, very hard, across the face. She may stumble. They both stare at each other, trying to figure out what this means for them.)

END OF PLAY

◎):IO

MARK BORKOWSKI *(Shadow Saint)*
Mark's plays have won critical acclaim from coast to coast. Most recently, *The Head Hunter* (The Producers Club) and *A Gravedigger's Tale* (The Hudson Guild). Other NYC productions include: *The Daughters of Eve* (The Cherry Lane Studio Theatre), *The Mutilation of St. Barbara* (The Gene Frankel Theatre), *Twilight's Child* (Playwright's Horizons), *Within the Skins of Saints* (The Common Basis Theatre), *The Rude Man* (The Kraine Theatre), *The Godling*, and *The Shadow Keeper* (Tribeca Lab), as well as many others. Outside New York: *Suicide, Inc.* at The Walnut St. Theatre. In Los Angeles, his *Lonely Vigil for a Stranger* ran at The Burbage Theatre where LA Times heralded it, "fireworks and poetry." Publications include: *A Gravedigger's Tale* (Smith & Krauss) "Best One Acts of 2009" and *Don't Listen to What It Sounds Like* (Smith & Krauss) "Best One Acts of 2007." He is the winner of the Playwrights Fellowship Award from the Pennsylvania Council of the Arts and The Rod Serling Award for *The Godling*. Also a screenwriter, his award winning thriller, *The Perfect Witness* is available on DVD worldwide, Netflix and on Showtime. Mark is a proud lifetime member of The Actors Studio and The Dramatists Guild.

ELEANOR BURGESS *(Park Slope Minstrel Show)*
Eleanor's plays have been produced by the Last Act Theatre Company, the Samuel French Off Off Broadway Festival, Everyday Inferno Theatre Company, the Emerging America Festival and the One Minute Play Festival. She has also had work read and developed at the Vineyard Theatre, New Georges, Broad Horizons, Reverie Productions, and the Crashbox Theater Company. She has been a playwriting fellow at the Huntington Theatre Company in Boston and a member of the writers' group at the Arcola Theatre in London. She is currently pursuing an MFA in Dramatic Writing at NYU's Tisch School of the Arts which will conclude in May of 2015.

PETER M. CARROZZO *(Key to My Heart)*
Peter is an attorney and adjunct professor. He has published law review articles, written numerous plays and created a website (www.constitutionland.com). This is his first staged production. "Thrilled, honored and humbled...many thanks to the *Collective:10*, Cassie, Dave and Maggie! Thanks to my wife Erin, and kids Katherine, Abigail and Patrick for love, support and laughs!"

BOB DeROSA *(Rocket Sex)*
Bob DeRosa is a proud member of Sacred Fools Theater Company in Los Angeles, CA, where he writes for ongoing shows *Serial Killers* and *Fast & Loose*. Bob also writes movies (*Killers*, *The Air I Breathe*) and television (*White Collar*). While his play *Rocket Sex* was being presented, he was honeymooning with his awesome wife Jen!

ROBERT Z GRANT (Editor– *C:10 Anthology*)
Robert is a founding member and Co-Artistic Director of The Collective and has taken on many roles with the company. Actor: Ionesco's *The Lesson*, *Café d'Automatique*; *The Brazilian Dilemma*, *Me Equals This*. Director: *Someone Who'll Watch Over Me* (2010 NYIT Award nomination for Outstanding Direction); *360 – An original adaptation of La Ronde*; *Faith on a Tuesday*, *Aunt Sylvia Is Dead*. Creative Director: The Collective website and publicity materials, and book designer and editor of the *C:10 Anthology - Volumes 1 and 2*. Playwright: *Outside The Box; Letting All the Air Out* (Top 10 finalist, Davenport 10-Minute Play Festival). As an improviser, Robert tours with the award-winning show *Broadway's Next H!T Musical* around New York and across the country, and teaches improvisation and acting. Robert attended NYU's Tisch School of the Arts and is also a graduate of the William Esper Studio where he studied with Bill Esper. Robert is probably best known for his anonymity. www.robertzgrant.com

ELIN HAMPTON *(Casey229)*
Ms. Hampton is an LA-based playwright, lyricist and TV writer/producer. Her work has been seen at The York Theatre Company, The Duplex, The Road Theatre Company, and the Hollywood Fringe Festival. Her play *The Bells of West 87th* recently had a sold out run at the Greenway Arts Alliance. *Amother Musical* (co-written with composer Gerald Sternbach) premiered at the Hudson Guild Backstage and is now licensed by Steele Spring Stage Rights and available on Amazon.com. Her television credits include "Mad About You," "Buffy the Vampire Slayer," "Dream On," "Pinky and the Brain," John Leguizamo's "House of Buggin'," and "The Gregory Hines Show." She is a proud member of: WGA, Dramatists Guild, ASCAP, TCG, ALAP, LAFPI, and EST Playwrights Unit.

STEPHEN HANCOCK *(4:00 A.M.: Redmond & Meda)*
Stephen received his MFA from The Pennsylvania State University. He joined the University of Memphis faculty as a full-time professor and member of the Performance Faculty, where he teaches classes in acting, directing, and playwriting. He serves as the Coordinator of the BFA Performance Program. Stephen is the author of several plays including *The Writer's Block*, *The Horror of the Little Family Farce*, *Revelations*, *The Lioness of the Leopards*, and *Zyrardów*. His plays have been performed or had staged readings in several cities including: NYC; New Orleans; Minneapolis; Jackson, MS; and Valdez, AK. He was runner-up in the 2005 Kennedy Center American College Theatre Festival David Mark Cohen Prize; is a two-time second-place winner of The Writer's Digest Magazine Writing Competition (Playwriting Division); and has twice been a semi-finalist in the Humana Festival 10-Minute play competition sponsored by Actors Theatre of Louisville. He has attended two of the country's most prestigious conferences for playwrights--The Sewanee Writers' Conference and The Prince William Sound Community College Edward Albee Last Frontier Theatre Conference--where he has studied with Edward Albee, Horton Foote, Marsha Norman, and Romulus Linney.

DAVE HANSON *(Cafe d'Automatique)*
Dave Hanson is an actor and writer living in New York City. Born in Seattle, WA, Dave studied theatre and writing at Whittier College in California and briefly attended The Oxford School of Drama at the University of Oxford. He spent several years in Los Angeles, working as an actor and writer, performing improv and sketch comedy (UCB LA, IO West, Second City LA) while touring the country as a stand up comedian. As a playwright Dave has written *Waiting for Waiting For Godot* (2013 FringeNYC Overall Excellence Award winner) and *The Exit Interview* (C:10 Play Festival). He is also a former writer and producer for *Chelsea Lately* (E!), *Beer:30* (Versus), and *Inside Sports* (Versus). Online writing credits include *Lonely Dave* (comedycentral.com), *Cubical of History* (funnyordie.com) as well as having several essays and short stories published in online publications. Recently Dave starred Off-Broadway as Val in *Waiting for Waiting For Godot* (2013 Fringe Fest & Encore Series), and was a New York Times Critic's Pick as Mike Regan in *The Boss* (Metropolitan Playhouse). Television & film credits: *The Onion News Network* (IFC), *Chelsea Lately* (E!), *The Ghost Whisperer* (CBS), *Scrubs* (NBC), *Carnivale* (HBO), *Sparks* (Sideshow productions), *Gamers* (Sideshow prod.).

LISA KICIELINSKI (Editor– *C:10 Anthology*)
Lisa K. is a permanent ensemble member and former Managing Director of The Collective and a development consultant, producer, and media scientist in NYC. With The Collective, she appeared in *Happy Girl*, *Burnt Toast*, and *Rocket Sex* and on *Inside Amy Schumer*. Actors Studio and Carnegie Mellon alum. Lisa produced the one-man comedy show *Cursing at Strangers* and is producing *Turtleface* for CollectiveNY Films. She's worked with Sidewalk and Dublin Film Festivals, Steeltown Entertainment, KDKA television station, HBO, and Skadden, Arps. She aims to use her love for scientific research and metrics to build communities around good stories. @LisaKhere

BRIAN LEIDER *(quick fix)*
As a founding member of The Collective, Brian is happy to work again with such a dynamic group of actors. He has worked as a writer, director and actor for theatre, film and television. Currently, he is planning to direct the film version of "quick fix" this winter. He would like to thank his partner in life, Caitlin Zvoleff, for her unconditional support, without which none of his work would be possible.

ERIN MALLON *(Good Working With Hands)*
Erin Mallon is an actor, writer and voice artist living in NYC. Her plays have been presented with Urban Stages, The American National Theatre, Last Frontier Theatre Conference, Hudson Valley Shakespeare Festival, Amios Theatre Company, The Collective, Cherry Picking, The Great Plains Theatre Conference, InViolet Theater and The Brooklyn Generator. Erin's play *Branched* directed by Robert Ross Parker and produced by InViolet Theater premiered at HERE Arts Center (February 2014). Recent work as an actor includes: Mac Wellman's solo show *Horrocks (and Toutatis too)* (Sleeping Weazel), Eric John Meyer's *The Sister* (Dutch Kills), multiple shows with Buran Theater, and Sara Farrington's plays *Requiem for Black Marie* (Incubator Arts Project), *Mickey and Sage* (Incubator Arts Project) and *Untitled Wharton Project* (JACK). Erin is also a devoted volunteer at The 52nd Street Project, the voice of many audiobooks and commercials and co-curator of The Brooklyn Generator. www.erinmallon.net

CRAIG McNULTY *(Watertown, Mass.)*
Craig has spent 30 years working in theatre, TV, and film as an actor, producer and playwright. His plays have been produced on four different continents and he has worked with genius and idiots. Some of the genius has been the ten plays of his done by The Collective and all the times he has gotten to work with Amy Wright. Complete life and fast artistic times can be found @ craigmcnulty.com. This play is dedicated to his mentor Julie McKee.

TERRY MILNER *(Nothing Is Free)*
Terry is a playwright and actor based in New York City. His full-length plays include *The Jesus Fund*, *Lawyers in Love* and *Adam Then*. A former attorney and nonprofit arts advocate, Terry is currently a second-year MFA candidate in Dramatic Writing at NYU's Tisch School of the Arts.

SAYRA PLAYER *(Uncle Silas)*
Sayra is a member of the Actors Studio and The Collective. She has extensive downtown theatre credits, and worked in Italy and Poland with the Workcenter of Jerzy Grotowski and Thomas Richards. Sayra was recently on "Inside Amy Schumer." She starred in Joe Maggio's *Paper Covers Rock* (IFC/ SXSW) and *Euphoria*. Other credits include: *A Little Closer*, *Pacing the Cage*, *Duane Hopwood* (Sundance), *How I Got Lost*, *Law and Order* and *The Song Still Inside*.

JENNY RACHEL WEINER *(Aunt Sylvia Is Dead)*
Jenny Rachel Weiner is a playwright and theatre artist currently residing in New York City. Plays include: *diventare* (KCACTF National Student Playwriting Award, In Cite Arts Festival @ New World Stages), *The Cave Play* (O'Neill Semi-Finalist), *The Selfish Giant* (Northlight Theatre, commission), *Horse Girls* (Fordham/Primary Stages, Ars Nova, Collaboraction; Chicago, upcoming: the cell, NYC; Annex Theatre; Seattle), *Nina* (Fordham/Primary Stages), *Jason&Julia* (Williamstown Theatre Festival) BFA: Boston University, MFA: Fordham University/ Primary Stages.

THE COLLECTIVE

www.thecollective-ny.org

○):10

ABOUT **THE COLLECTIVE**

THE COLLECTIVE unites professional artists who share a responsibility to create work in the contemporary American Theatre that is emotionally truthful, socially relevant, and defiantly accessible. The company was established in the tradition of the Group Theatre out of a belief that the current conditions of commercialized theatre necessitate collective action. Commitment to a permanent ensemble distinguishes The Collective. Through a shared vocabulary, uniform technique, and continual practice, the group pursues a common purpose: to establish a theatre that is uncompromising, relevant, and inclusive.

The Collective began in 2007, when several recent graduates of the William Esper Studio came together to continue to create and produce work that built on their recent training and the strengths and talents of their colleagues. The parting advice to many of the graduates was to 'create your own work' as a way of taking control over one's career. The Collective exists to provide a network and a place where these individuals can showcase their talents.

Eugène Ionesco's classic absurdist comedy *The Lesson* was The Collective's first stage production, and was presented at Center Stage, NY in the Fall of 2007. The response from audiences and colleagues was incredibly positive, and interest in The Collective increased ten-fold. The immediate question became: 'What are you doing next?' Maura O'Brien of *Off Off Online* noted in her review of the production: "*The Lesson* is The Collective's first production... It's exciting to think about how the group will apply such fierce energy to other works."

Since then, The Collective has produced ten plays and five Collective Comedy shows (*Time Out New York* Critics' Pick). The group co-produced a short film festival and shot a short film, and helped develop a series for Comedy Central, as well as numerous screenplays. The Collective continues to actively pursue and develop new work.

Active members of The Collective Permanent Ensemble are: Patrick Bonck, Karen Chamberlain, Margaret Champagne, Victoria Dicce (founding member), John D'Ornellas, Booker Garrett, Robert Z Grant (founding member, Co-Artistic Director), Swann Gruen, Dave Hanson, Mike Houston (founding member), Kevin Kane (founding member, Co-Artistic Director), Lisa Kicielinski, Nina Mehta, Khalil Muhammad, Sayra Player, and Amy Schumer (founding member).

NO EMPTY SEATS – The Collective "Make Theatre Accessible" Initiative

The Collective is a not-for-profit production company. We rely on the generosity of our supporters to continue to produce top-quality theatre and film, and to foster our development of emerging writers.

Through our NO EMPTY SEATS initiative, up to HALF the seats for each performance are made available on a FREE and pay-what-you-can basis. For **Collective:10**, **every $10 = one seat** that we were able to make available for FREE to someone who could not afford a ticket to quality professional theatre or did not previously know that such opportunities exist. We would rather perform for an enthusiastic and engaged audience who has not paid a dime than to have one empty seat.

You can participate in NO EMPTY SEATS in three ways:

Buy a ticket to see a performance.
Make a donation so that a free seat can be made available for someone else.
Fill a seat for free, or pay-what-you-can.

Your tax-deductible* contribution, however large or small, will help ensure that we can continue our mission.

For more information and to make a donation:
www.no-empty-seats.org

Mark, where are you from?

Philadelphia.

How long have you been writing?

Since I was a kid.

Where did the idea for *Shadow Saint* come from?
A few years ago, I was bottoming out on drugs and finally waking up to the predicament I was in. I wanted to find a metaphor for the awakening I experienced. At first, it came out in the form of a monologue, which I performed at poetry readings in New York and LA. Then, one night, I started to hear voices around it and it became a play.

What question is *Shadow Saint* trying to answer?

Does a human being have the right to force an awakening on someone? (My answer is 'no'.)

What is the real challenge of writing a ten-minute play?

Confining the experience or a piece of the experience so that the audience feels a life before and after the event. The technical challenge is taking that experience and applying the 3 act structure so there's a beginning, middle and end.

What draws you to this form of storytelling?

It's like writing a song as opposed to an opera. Or a short story instead of a novel. A prayer as opposed to a mass. Some stories only need a few minutes to be told, others eternity isn't enough.

Who or what are your artistic influences?

I'm particularly turned on by the classics. Not just playwrights but also great fiction and poetry. Music is an incredible source that also feeds my writing. I tend to read and listen to music that lends itself to what I'm working on. For instance, I'm currently working on something that is seasoned with Hinduism, so I find myself drawn to Kirtan music and the Ramayana.

What projects next excite you?

I just finished my play *Vesey Street* which was just read at The Actors Studio. We're in the process of finding a theatre for it (hint-hint). I'm, at present, finishing another play, *Playing with Shadows* which is the full length version of *Shadow Saint*. As a screenwriter, my screenplay "The Last Verse" (based on 'The Tibetan Book of the Dead') is in pre-production and slated to shoot in the Spring of 2015.

Peter, where are you from?

Flushing, Queens.

How long have you been writing?

My writing career began in fifth grade; I wrote a skit in a school play that stole heavily from the Marx Brothers and Bugs Bunny. My other works from that era include a game show sketch called "Truth or Death"...mildly amusing today, but hysterical at 11 years old. In high school my English teacher Mrs. Monson read my satirical short story entitled "The Assassination of Tom Carvel" to the class and said that someday I would be an author—her enthusiasm for my writing still motivates me today. Since then I've written short stories, sketches in school (law school follies), bad haikus, several published law review articles, goofy comments on Facebook, websites on legal issues (including www.constitutionland. com, a virtual amusement park for people who love the US Constitution) and lots of plays—my favorite genre. As a result I have a voluminous and varied collection of rejection letters which I keep in a big file cabinet as a constant motivation to keep writing. Most of my writing takes place secretly—either while hiding from work pretending to be working or hiding from the world pretending to be participating.

Where did the idea for *Key to My Heart* come from?

Most of my plays come from desires, dilemmas or conflicts. I like to put likable people that I know well and understand into odd situations. Then, as they struggle, suffer or succeed, I jot down the minutes of the proceedings I hear in my mind and hopefully turn it into a play. The idea for *Key to My Heart* came from a question from my imagination: what if two normal and pretty square people find themselves at the front door of an unconventional house party? When I realized why these morally good people were standing at this front door, I knew I could tell their story truthfully without compromising the personalities I created for them.

What question is *Key to My Heart* trying to answer?

Can love overcome pride, ego, and the conflicts and nonsense of everyday life?

What is the real challenge of writing a ten-minute play?

How do you create three dimensional characters that the audience can relate to and care about and tell an entire story in just ten minutes? The temptation is to throw in a trick or unrealistic or dishonest twist in an attempt to say something important quickly. The most important thing you can say in a play, be it ten minutes or otherwise, is the truth.

What draws you to this form of storytelling?

I love trying to tell an entire story and create a universe of humanity in ten short minutes. It's like playing a game of chess, or doing the Saturday *New York Times* crossword puzzle in less than five minutes. And if the audience cares about and wants to know more about these characters, I'm very happy.

Who or what are your artistic influences?

I love reading plays and books about writers. I've read everything Neil Simon has ever written, including his autobiography. His writing style and his explanation of the creative process and necessity for rewriting are my greatest influence. I also love Meredith Willson's autobiography on writing and staging *The Music Man*...an ode to perseverance. My favorite playwrights and authors include Arthur Miller, Tennessee Williams, August Wilson, Woody Allen, Robert Benchley, Herman Wouk, Carl Reiner and Mel Brooks. My absolute favorite writing is anything where someone says a lot while saying absolutely nothing...like in *The Catcher in the Rye*, *The Sun Also Rises*, and *Pulp Fiction*. And I'm heavily influenced by that painting of those dogs playing poker!

What projects next excite you?

I am hooked on writing ten-minute plays but some of these are slowly becoming one act plays. I am also in various stages on two full-length plays. In one play, I am currently at the stage where I stare at page 14 and say now what? Someday, I would love to write a series of historical plays (combining my love of legal history and theater) but I am frozen by the thought of writing dialogue from a different era. I hope to give it a try, though. Whatever happens, I will keep on writing...even if it's sketches for the Shady Rest Retirement Home in the year 2062!

Bob, where are you from?

I grew up in Orlando, Florida. I fell in love with filmmaking at the University of Florida and after I graduated, returned home to take advantage of what was being promoted as "Hollywood East." It didn't live up to the hype, but it did create an amazing community of artists, writers, directors, and actors. I made short films, co-founded the award-winning sketch and improv comedy troupe THEM, wrote and directed short plays, and worked for the Florida Film Festival. It was an incredible time and after the *Orlando Weekly* voted me Renaissance Man (for real) I moved to Los Angeles.

How long have you been writing?

I wrote my first short story when I was six. The rights to *The Baby Dragon* are still available. When I moved to L.A., I decided to put all my focus into screenwriting while doing improv on the side. When my troupe went on hiatus, I started writing one-acts and late-night serials for Sacred Fools Theater and that's been my creative home ever since.

Where did the idea for *Rocket Sex* come from?

Sacred Fools does a show called Fast & Loose, where writers are given two parameters and a cast breakdown and tasked with writing a one-act overnight. The next day, a director and actors are chosen at random and the show goes up that night. I was writing for the New Year's Eve show two years ago and my variables were "porn theater" and "private space exploration." I came up with two ideas that had nothing to do with each other and wondered if it was possible to somehow combine them. This play is the result.

What is the real challenge of writing a ten-minute play?

Making it a full story and not just a fleshed-out scene. It doesn't matter how long or short something is, if you're in a theater and the lights go up and some stuff happens and then the lights go down, you want that stuff to matter. Making it matter and having only ten minutes to do it isn't exactly easy. I find insane deadlines help.

What draws you to this form of storytelling?

Honestly, the speed of it all. I've made a living as a screenwriter in Hollywood for over ten years now and I've gotten two movies made. The wait for a project to happen is excruciating. I love writing for theater because I can dream up something one night, and then see actors bring it to life the next day. It's pretty intoxicating.

Who or what are your artistic influences?

I'm not one of those guys who idolizes one particular artist. I've stolen bits and pieces from so many influences: writers, bands, filmmakers. When it comes to theater, I'm inspired by actors, pure and simple. I've been to film festivals and Fringe festivals all over the continent, and if I had to choose, I'd rather be in a beer tent full of actors any day of the week.

What projects next excite you?

I'm co-creating a web-series with my good friend Ben Rock called *20 Seconds to Live* (follow us at @20STL). I have a new TV pilot going out soon, so ask me in two months if I'm excited about it or not. And I really, really need to write a full-length play. It's been taunting me for years.

Elin, where are you from?

I grew up in a small town on Long Island: Old Bethpage. But I spent much of my formative years in New England, often summering in Cape Cod, and got my theatre degree from the University of Vermont.

How long have you been writing?

I started writing for New York cabaret shows in which I performed during the 80s. In 1990, I moved to Los Angeles and soon found myself writing for television, beginning with Roseanne and Tom Arnold's "The Jackie Thomas Show." I returned to writing for the stage in my spare time about ten years later.

Where did the idea for *Casey229* come from?

I've always been intrigued by stories of lonely people creating virtual identities for themselves on social media, carrying on relationships that exist purely in the ether of the Internet -- and wondered how far one could take this manufactured reality.

What question is *Casey229* trying to answer?

If this is the new normal in human interaction, might there be something positive and valuable to come out of it? Is it possible that people's avatars speak more honestly, because they have less to lose?

What is the real challenge of writing a ten-minute play?

The biggest challenge is to craft characters and flesh out the premise enough to transcend just being a sketch. Finding the pathos and heart of a story in such a short time is a great exercise.

What draws you to this form of storytelling?

I've grown to love the limitation of the very specific page count. There are ten-minute festivals being done all over the country, providing a great opportunity for playwrights to introduce themselves and for theater companies that may not read unsolicited full-length scripts to discover fresh, new voices.

Who or what are your artistic influences?

So many everyday things can inspire me: a newspaper article, a conversation overheard in Starbucks, or in a waiting room... They may all find their way into my writing. My heroes of the theater include Annie Baker, Sarah Ruhl, Yasmina Reza, Christopher Durang, Neil Simon and Stephen Sondheim.

What projects next excite you?

In addition to my first feature-length screenplay, I'm working on a new one-act I hope to premiere in Los Angeles early next year. Fingers crossed.

Brian, where are you from?

Just outside the middle of nowhere: Grayslake, IL.

How long have you been writing?

Since birth.

Where did the idea for *quick fix* come from?

The death of a role model.

What question is *quick fix* trying to answer?

How does one live fully, one day at a time?

What is the real challenge of writing a ten-minute play?

Reducing a complete, life-changing event to 10 minutes.

What draws you to this form of storytelling?

Nothing: the short form is too difficult, but sometimes an idea hits you and you have no choice.

Who or what are your artistic influences?

My mother is the origin of both need and ability to create.

What projects next excite you?

I'm working to adapt and direct a film version of *quick fix* this winter.

Erin, where are you from?

Warminster, PA (right outside of Philadelphia).

How long have you been writing?

I'm a long time actor and have been secretly scribbling in notebooks for years, though I started writing in earnest and putting things in actors' mouths about four years ago.

Where did the idea for *Good Working With Hands* come from?
I originally wrote *Good Working With Hands* as part of The Brooklyn Generator, a monthly project I created and now co-curate with Bixby Elliot. We focus on full-length plays now, but used to write ten-minute plays sparked from a theme. The theme that particular month was "insane Bible verses." The verse I pulled out of the hat had to do with how a man treats his slave. Somehow this led me to writing this play. Because they're slaves to their job? To each other? Who knows! The creative process is a wily little critter.

What question is *Good Working With Hands* trying to answer?

How do you survive a relationship where you love and hate the other person in equal measure?

What is the real challenge of writing a ten-minute play?

A few years ago, I read this great essay by Jon Jory about the power of the ten-minute play. He likened it to a firecracker. It explodes, burns bright for a short time and then dies quickly. I loved that and try to remember that whenever I write one. With only ten minutes, you don't have much time for build-up or exposition, so you gotta get right to the juicy stuff (not a bad idea for a play of any length!) and make every moment count.

Who or what are your artistic influences?

I'm a big fan of Peter Sinn Nachtrieb and Nicky Silver's work. I love how they're able to create absurd people and circumstances and keep you laughing the whole time while still treading in some super dark waters.

What projects next excite you?

I'm currently developing my new full-length play *The Other White Meat* which takes place on a "compassionate farm" where people aren't particularly compassionate. Talking animals, Crossfit ballets, and menstruation ceremonies abound! I'm also diving into work on my new solo show exploring sex, religion, feminism and theme parks.

Craig, where are you from?

I was born in the great Borough of Queens in the same hospital Cyndi Lauper was born in- my family moved to upstate New York where I grew up in the Hudson Valley, Orange County (the real OC bitches). I moved to Brooklyn in 1993 and lived in five different Brooklyn 'hoods over the next fifteen years. I now live in Manhattan, So when I say "I'm a New Yorker," it's no bullshit.

How long have you been writing?

Very seriously for ten years. (This month [October 2014] is actually exactly ten years of throwing myself intensely at writing.) I had the urge to write since high school but it wasn't until Fall of 2004 that I joined the best writing class in the city- Julie McKee's writing workshop at HB Studio and found the moral courage to write (and the craft by which to do it well). In her class, the one sentence "write for the wastebasket" freed me like nothing else ever has-- if you're writing for the "wastebasket," doesn't matter if it sucks or not- what matters is that you write, and if you write enough and re-write with clarity and honesty then some of it will actually avoid the wastebasket and might get performed. Maybe even by brilliant artists like those of The Collective, if you're lucky. I've been very lucky.

Where did the idea for *Watertown, Mass.* come from?

The week of the Boston Marathon bombings, when days later the two assholes who did the crime were being chased around Watertown and the area, the entire greater Boston area was put on lockdown. People were stuck wherever they were for the entire day and not really knowing when it would end. I read a blog by a particularly banal writer who basically bragged about how he was at the apartment of a gal who he had a friend-with-benefits type of deal and nothing interesting happened other than them hanging out watching TV. The point of the article seemed to be he was bragging that he has sex. Wow. BFD. What occurred to me is how much more loaded the situation would be if it was an alcohol-fueled hookup where two people wake up having had an extremely intense physical interaction (hot sex) but knowing nothing really about each other, and how they would have to navigate this very bizarre set of circumstances. My teacher and friend, Austin Pendleton, would often tell us in acting class that in any great (or even just competent) play that the characters should have such loaded "given circumstances" that the scene that takes place simply *must* happen.

What question is *Watertown, Mass.* trying to answer?

How do we choose to live our lives in the era of terrorist attacks on our homeland and specifically on our hometowns?

I think people can go in many different directions- I know I did. On 9/11, I was out of town on my way back into NYC- my train was turned around and since I was the only person on the train with a transistor radio, I was relaying an impossible-to-comprehend series of events. (Of the many things that stood out was me trying to convince an elderly woman that the entire South Tower did actually collapse- she kept telling me this was impossible, it must have been just a large piece of the building- I ended up getting very short with her as I told her that this was something that Peter Jennings would not be making up.) My apartment in the Cobble Hill section of Brooklyn was right on the water on Columbia street with no structures separating the World Trade Center and my building- when the collapse did happen much of the debris drifted across the river and ended up covering my neighborhood.

When I got back to NYC a few days later, my world was different and I dealt with shit by throwing myself for the next few months (depending on the day you were around me) into Catholicism, Hedonism, Buddhism, Happy Hours that served food, Ashtanga Yoga for sometimes three hours a day, advocating nuclear war on the Middle East, wanting to join Peace Corps, inquiring about joining the Armed Forces, looking to volunteer at Ground Zero, considering leaving the country, or moving to a desert or the hills- and all this on no sleep. For weeks. Literally. I would go on 10- to 20-mile walks around the City 'cause I was unemployed and did it in an attempt to make myself tired. I had sex at 3 a.m. in the middle of the Brooklyn Bridge with some English woman I met at midnight. (We told ourselves that this was some great act of defiance as the Brooklyn Bridge was definitely a terrorist target and somehow fucking each other was saying 'fuck you' to Al Qaeda- at the time this made sense... I guess you had to be there.) There are days that I completely blacked out. Fall of 2001 and others live in incredibly vivid detail in my mind.

Thirteen years post 9/11 and in this play (about the Boston bombings) and in many others I wrote (including *Pink Dress* and *may first twenty eleven*, both produced by The Collective and directed by Maggie Champagne), the question is when these senseless acts of extreme violence happen, how do we choose to live the rest of our lives? Sometimes I'm all *carpe noctem*-- make the most of every minute; sometimes I think what's the point of all this struggle when your life can disappear for no goddamn reason at all? In *Watertown, Mass.*, both characters represent my many sides in struggling with these questions. Maybe if I keep writing about people struggling with these same issues, I'll find my answers. This is why I had to write this play.

What is the real challenge of writing a ten-minute play?

Finding a situation that is interesting and engaging, but being finite enough that there can be a satisfying conclusion at page 10. Fine line between being clever and being stupid.

What draws you to this form of storytelling?

Mark Borkowski [writer of *Shadow Saint* in this volume] felt the difference between writing a short story and writing a poem is that in a poem you get to really shout- and then it's over. And while a ten-minute play is longer than a poem, it's a helluva lot shorter than a full-length play and in the ten-minute form you can really unload with both barrels and then: Bang! Boom! It's over!

Who or what are your artistic influences?

Paul Auster, Charles Bukowski, Martin McDonagh, Werner Herzog, Oliver Stone, Richard Price, Lanford Wilson, John Patrick Shanley, Lem Dobbs and Sparkles Biederman.

What projects next excite you?

A play, *Something In The Night*, I wrote and developed for many years at Collective Mondays, and I'm very proud of. Thrilled about working on a film adaptation of my play *Welcome Home Steve*. Continuing development with a Chicago company, Revolution Theatre, on a play *Black Hearted Love*, and re-booting a play I've worked on for many years on and off called *Night Vision* about a soldier coming home from Iraq that is a good play, but it just didn't feel as urgent or necessary as it should be -- a few weeks ago I realized having a female protagonist made it both urgent and necessary and something I wanted to work on. When I have the impulse that I have to get to my MacBook Air to get down what's in my head, life is good.

Q&A WITH THE PLAYWRIGHTS:
TERRY MILNER
Nothing Is Free

Terry, where are you from?

I was born in Jackson, Mississippi, but I've lived all over the country. This is my third time living in New York.

How long have you been writing?

Seven years, more or less, though not full-time by any means. I started to write in something like a serious way in 2007, which is when I wrote the first draft of my first full-length, *The Jesus Fund*, and another (still unfinished) play soon followed. When I got offered a production of *The Jesus Fund* by a theatre in North Carolina, that gave me some confidence, so I started applying to serious MFA programs and got into my first choice, which was Tisch.

Where did the idea for *Nothing Is Free* come from?
I wrote it as part of a writing exercise in Annie Baker's workshop at NYU. We were given a set of restrictions regarding setting and character, but otherwise were free to write whatever came to mind. So I wrote the first draft in about two hours. The idea for an absurdist piece came to me after seeing the wonderful *Waiting For Godot* on Broadway last season, which made me think about how we live in a similar time to the period in which the major absurdists (Beckett, Ionesco, etc.) were writing, and how the same absurdist themes of the loss of personal agency and control might apply to our day and age.

What question is *Nothing Is Free* trying to answer?

How far are we willing to go in order to guarantee continued access to seemingly free or really cheap consumer goods? How much personal agency and human connection are we as a species willing to surrender to technology, globalization, and the corporate hegemony before we decide enough is enough, and dare to look away from the video screen and into each other's eyes again?

What is the real challenge of writing a ten-minute play?

Traditional dramatic storytelling comes in three parts, in which the playwright is expected to set up a situation, disrupt a situation through conflict and change, then resolve it. Getting that arc across in ten minutes means you have almost no margin for waste or error. You have very little time for the setup, i.e., establishing the characters' status quo and their basic motivating desires. So that has to happen by page 2 or 3 at the latest, so you spend the rest of the time on the exciting stuff: seeing how the characters strive, fail, and strive again, and how that all turns out for them. So it's really a matter of making sure your writing is as economical as possible without giving up character development and story.

What draws you to this form of storytelling?

Ten-minute plays are in some ways like the haikus of playwriting. Not as strictly governed by convention, of course, but certainly shorter than most. Because of this brevity, I think you get to leave more questions unanswered, because you simply don't have time to answer them all. So in that way it feels almost like a poem.

Who or what are your artistic influences?

In terms of other art forms, I love the early paintings of Kandinsky: the dark, expressionistic landscapes make me want to go there with him as a writer. I love Harold Pinter's plays. Sadly, most of us are first introduced to Pinter as literature, and when you're an only slightly above-average high school student like I was, you can easily dismiss him as unreadable. But once I had the chance to act in a Pinter play as an undergrad, and then saw some of his films (check out *Turtle Diary*, just beautiful), I realized, he's just writing really, really specific, honest, hyper-naturalistic dialogue.

What projects next excite you?

I just finished a solid draft of play that I am so happy about and so in love with. I've recently submitted it to development conferences and workshops and hope that some of them will help me get it ready for production by the end of next year. It's a pretty simple scenario: a group of people on vacation together in France. But they are all forced to confront some serious problems and dilemmas, and they are all tested, as you can often be when cooped up in paradise with people you don't know very well. But there's a swimming pool on stage, and casting requires a set of adult male twins, so the odds of it ever getting produced are pretty long. But I am so in love with it, and that's not always the case with me and my work.

:10

Sayra, where are you from?

Independence, Missouri.

How long have you been writing?

Around ten years of dabbling. I am an actress who writes when there is no project, and until my daughter was born, there was always a distraction, so completing writing was never a priority. I would go from one unfinished screenplay or play to the next. Now that I am unable to act for a while as I take care of her, I am finding time to complete stories for a change.

Where did the idea for *Uncle Silas* come from?

I have a question that lingers in me about how I could have helped the addicts I love in my life more. I feel for those whose worst fears come true and the addiction takes away that someone from them for good.

What question is *Uncle Silas* trying to answer?

What can you do to help someone who is risking it all? What happens when you try your very best to help them make a change? What is the cost of self-destructing?

What is the real challenge of writing a ten-minute play?

I like the limitation, the challenge of finding what is essential, making a story and people's history that could fill pages then boiling it down to ten minutes with nothing missing and nothing spelled out.

What draws you to this form of storytelling?

I want to be obsessive and fudge with every little nuance. I started writing this in January, and have continually made changes. It is small enough that I can feel it is almost exactly what I want to express.

Who or what are your artistic influences?

I have too many. Charlie Chaplin's heart and humor. I feel like a tragic clown and see that humor in everyone I meet and write. My next play will be funny. Lars Von Trier's aesthetic and expectation for his actors to give themselves wholly. Ellen Burstyn, Estelle Parsons and Elizabeth Kemp are my acting mentors, and I cherish all I have learned from them.

What projects next excite you?

I will finish the dark comedy about my mother's life as a cleaning lady in conservative, paranoid Missouri.

Jenny, where are you from?

I grew up in South Florida, went to college in Boston, lived in Chicago for a few years, and now am based in New York City.

How long have you been writing?

I have been writing seriously since my senior year of college in 2009; I went to school for acting, but began taking classes with Lydia Diamond and found myself really excited by writing plays. Boston University produced my first play *diventare* in 2010, which went on to win the Kennedy Center/American College Theatre Festival's National Student Playwriting Award, and I haven't really stopped since.

Where did the idea for *Aunt Sylvia Is Dead* come from?

When my Farfar (father's father in Swedish) passed away five years ago, I found myself not only grieving, but also oddly amused and fascinated by my family dynamic. I remember my Dad and I sitting in the waiting room while they were about to pull my Farfar off of life support, incredulous at our family's wild behavior, and whispering to each other "this is a play!" Old wounds came seeping to the surface, grief and sadness turned to anger and aggression, but at the heart of it all was just a family needing each other to feel seen, to be hugged, and to be given permission to be vulnerable.

What question is your play trying to answer?

I think my play answers the question: what happens to our family dynamic when the Matriarch leaves us? Who takes over the role of caretaker, of peacekeeper, of unconditional lover? I think at the heart of the play is a family clinging to old beliefs and old ways of being because they are afraid of what's to come—but, what they really want all along, is to feel seen and loved by their family in the face of grief.

What is the real challenge of writing a ten-minute play?

I think it's easy to make a ten-minute play feel sparse or one dimensional; creating characters that feel full and dynamic, with strong wants and needs, is difficult in such a short amount of time, but because of the ten-minute container, can also be a gift because it forces us to get right to the heart of the matter.

What draws you to this form of storytelling?

I love writing plays that are emotional, active, explosive. I aim to create a world that doesn't let you go, that never allows you to drift away and wonder what you'll eat for dinner, that keeps the audience present with each other and the story. The ten-minute form is a perfect space for that kind of high-frequency storytelling.

Who or what are your artistic influences?

I am inspired by writers like Paula Vogel, Sheila Callaghan, Annie Baker, Jill Solloway—women who are writing vulnerable, funny, honest stories about people we can identify with. These women hold up a mirror so that we can see ourselves reflected back, see our deepest selves, see our darkest selves, see the questions we want to ask the world, see the things in the world that make us angry, that make us feel excited, that call us into action.

PERMISSIONS ACKNOWLEDGMENTS

C):10

THE COLLECTIVE
TEN MINUTE PLAY FEST

featuring new short plays by

Mark Borkowski   Peter M. Carrozzo   Bob DeRosa   Elin Hampton

Stephen Hancock   Dave Hanson   Brian Leider   Erin Mallon

Craig McNulty   Terry Milner   Sayra Player   Jenny Rachel Weiner

executive producers
Patrick Bonck   Victoria Dicce   Robert Z Grant   Mike Houston

lighting design   sound design   costume consultant
Maria Cristina Fuste   Mark Parenti   Amanda Jenks

production stage manager   assistant stage manager
Olivia Gemelli   Meghan Lynch

and contributions from
Members and Colleagues of The Collective

An Equity-approved showcase

THE COLLECTIVE "Make Theatre Accessible" mission

NO EMPTY SEATS

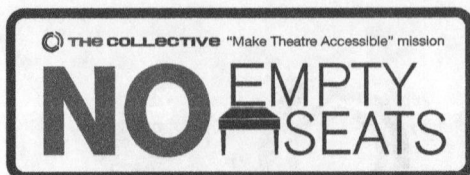

BUY TICKETS • MAKE A DONATION • FILL A SEAT

Thank you to our growing list of generous donors
for joining us in our mission to create access
to professional quality theater for all.

Collective:10
No Empty Seats Sponsors

Bryson & Sayra Brodie
Anne Elliott
Anonymous

Collective:10 Play Sponsors

Jane Baum • Rebecca Lynn Brillhart • Patrick Houston
Milton Nasajon • Ken & Mary Ann Zwaschka • Anonymous

Collective:10 Donors

Patricia Beaury • Michael Benjamin • Bonnie Brennan • Contemporary Laser
Albert Cooper • Jessah Diaz • Bill & Suzanne Esper • Rodney Fetaya
Frederick Freyer • Helen and Sandor Genet • Stephanie Goldman • Brayndi Grassi
Brian Hotaling • Amanda Ihlenfeld • Zak Mulligan • Shawlini Manjunath
Jaime Nasajon • Dan Powell • Holly Riedel • JB Roté • Greig Sargent
Lipica Shah • Nandita Shenoy • Brandon T. Snider • Karen Zechowy • Anonymous

SUPPORT NO EMPTY SEATS
with your donation

www.no-empty-seats.org

C:10